T0199151

Also by James M. Riccitelli

PUBLICATIONS

You May Now Kiss the Bride: Biblical Principles for Lifelong Marital Happiness (2012). WestBow Press, Bloomington. Indiana (240 pages)

"Pastor to Pastor, The Church's Music," (1998). H. B. London interviews Paul Walker, Gloria Gaither, Jack Hayford, and James Riccitelli (audio recording). *Focus on the Family, Vol. 35.*

Sing a New Song - When Music Divides the Church (1997). H & E Berk, Blissfield, MI (175 pages). Copies available from the author, Tel. 239-322-7661 or 419-699-3678; E-mail, bethanyjmr@aol.com

Parents' Rights vs. Professionals' Rights in Education, (1984). In David Tavel (Eds.), *Modern Education Controversies* (159-174). Lanham, New York, London: University Press of America.

Musical Taste and Social Experience: An Examination of Factors Related to the Enjoyment of Hard Rock and Heavy Classical Music among Students (1978). Copies available at the University of Toledo and Nyack College, Nyack, New York.

"Tone Analysis: A Practical Approach," (April 1965). *The Bible Translator. 16* (2), 54-73. http://www.ubs-translations.org/bt/

Developing Non-Western Hymnody. (November-December 1962) *Practical Anthropology, 9(6)*, 241-256.

RADIO

2009-2012 - "In the Classroom," a 15-minute weekly radio study program on biblical subjects; mp3 audio copies available at bathostheos.com/blog

1968-2014 — a 5-minute daily Bible reading program (1968-1978); then an updated program called *"Comment,"* that discussed current events from a biblical perspective (1978-2012). The programs are available on the author's blog at http://bathostheos.com.

Reviews

"James Riccitelli has stood on the shoreline and seen the tides come and go. In this book, he takes that perspective of decades of sociological experience and applies it to an understanding of authentic salvation. While the good news of the Gospel is not new, the old, old story is applied by Riccitelli to a new generation of believers resulting in a foundational knowledge for their faith."

- Dr. Russell L. Huizing
Assistant Professor of Pastoral Ministry, Toccoa Falls College

---

"I too see a lacking in my sons' walk and understanding of God's Word. I have read the first few chapters of Authenticate Your Faith, Here's How and Why and better understand where they are, and where we are as a Church - ouch! And yet there is a good word of challenge for me, too! As I drove to the home of Stateside relatives, I was able to share with two of my sons what I had been reading. - Thank you."

-From an International Worker on furlough with sons in college in the USA

"Thank you for a copy of your latest book. I've already started reading it and appreciate your unique perspective."

- Pastor Christian Becker

"You've struck the nail solidly on the head. Once you sit at the Lord's Table and get a large helping of the Word, you'll crave more. You'll tend to read your Bible during the week, and you'll devour the leftovers from the Sunday sermon."

- William L. Emery, Layman

Authenticate
Your
Faith

Here's How and Why

JAMES M. RICCITELLI

WESTBOW
PRESS®
A DIVISION OF THOMAS NELSON
& ZONDERVAN

Kenda M. Lentz with Lentz Photography for Figures 1-5

WestBow Press books may be ordered through booksellers or by contacting:

WestBow Press
A Division of Thomas Nelson & Zondervan
1663 Liberty Drive
Bloomington, IN 47403
www.westbowpress.com
1 (866) 928-1240

ISBN: 978-1-5127-5606-7 (sc)
ISBN: 978-1-5127-5607-4 (hc)
ISBN: 978-1-5127-5605-0 (e)

Library of Congress Control Number: 2016915017

Print information available on the last page.

WestBow Press rev. date: 11/21/2016

A LEGACY

FOR MY CHILDREN,

Kevin, Karis, Karen, Keith and Kenda,

for their

children and

children's children,

and for all

God's children everywhere

that all may know God more intimately,

become increasingly

biblically literate

and be confident of their salvation

in Jesus Christ.

I gave you milk to drink, not solid food;
for you were not yet able to receive it.
Indeed, even now you are not yet able.
Paul writing to the Corinthian Church
1 Corinthians 3:2

Concerning [Melchizedek] we have much to say,
and it is hard to explain,
since you have become dull of hearing.
For though by this time you ought to be teachers,
you have need again for someone to teach you
the elementary principles of the oracles of God,
and you have come to need milk and not solid food.
Everyone who partakes only of milk
is not accustomed to the word of righteousness,
for he is an infant.
But solid food is for the mature,
who because of practice have their senses trained
to discern good and evil.
Hebrews 5:11-14

"Americans revere the Bible — but, by and large, they don't read it. And because they don't read it, they have become a nation of biblical illiterates."

George Gallup and Jim Castelli
Researchers

✟ ✟ ✟ ✟ ✟

"How bad is it? Researchers tell us that it's worse than most could imagine."

Albert Mohler
President, Southern Baptist Convention

ACKNOWLEDGEMENTS

I am deeply indebted and truly grateful for the unstinting service of retired English teacher Jane Marton who graciously served as proofreader. She not only proofread the text but also made valuable suggestions on content. She penned at the end of one chapter, "Well done!" and at the end of another, "Good chapter!" At the end of Chapter 9, "Baptized in the Spirit," she wrote, "Yes! Well done — good explanation!!"

I am also exceedingly grateful for the hours that Kenda M. Lentz, PhD (my daughter) spent editing the manuscript. Her keen eye and commitment to stay with the editing—even though it took her into the late hours of the night —are very much appreciated.

A special thank you to Victor Oliver, PhD for suggesting the title and subtitle for this book and to Sharon Bruen for her skillful proofreading.

TABLE OF CONTENTS

Preface xix

Prologue: Vitals Report xxiii

Chapter 1   Introducing the Man From Nazareth *aka* Podunk................ 1

Chapter 2   Introducing the Man From Heaven *aka* His Father's House 15

Chapter 3   Salvation! Perfect Timing!.. 29

Chapter 4   Saved! 39

Chapter 5   Saved From Sin!..51

Chapter 6   Saved From Self!..61

Chapter 7   Saved From the Wrath of God!.. 89

Chapter 8   First Step of Obedience...103

Chapter 9   Baptized *in* the Holy Spirit 119

Chapter 10   Filled with the Spirit - *Gifts* 131

Chapter 11   Filled with the Spirit - *Fruit* 145

Chapter 12   Assurance of Salvation 155

Epilogue: How Authentic Is Your Faith? 167

Self-Assessment 175

About the Author...201

List of Figures

Figure 1. Unbeliever 59

Figure 2. Believer 60

Figure 3. Sanctified believer: The Act of Sanctification 86

Figure 4. Sanctified believer: The Process of Sanctification 87

Figure 5. Glorified believer 102

ABBREVIATIONS

English Standard Version	ESV
King James Version	KJV
New American Standard Bible Version	NASB
New International Version	NIV
New King James Version	NKJV
New Living Translation	NLT

PREFACE

Authenticate Your Faith!
Au·then·ti·cate, verb \ə-then-ti-kat\

"to prove that something is real, true, or genuine:
to prove that something is authentic"

- Merriam-Webster Dictionary

This book lays out the how and why of authenticating your faith. Let me turn those around and deal first with the "why" in the Preface and the Prologue. The remainder of the book will deal with the "how." Jumping right into the "why," let me start by asking some questions: Is your faith real, true, and genuine? Can you prove it is authentic? The answer depends on what you have been eating. That sounds like a strange answer, but it isn't.

If you lack physical strength and make an appointment with your physician, he may start with this question, "What are your eating habits?" That's not so bizarre since he suspects you are someone who snacks and are too busy to stop for meals. You answer honestly, "I drink a glass of milk for breakfast, another glass for lunch, and a third glass for supper." The doctor, wondering if he heard everything, asks, "And what else?" You reply, "That's it."

The doctor does not seem to be buying that answer, so you add defensively, "Milk is all they fed me when I was a baby, and I survived!" At this point, the doctor tries to recall the phone number of a nutritionist, thinking, "This patient needs help!"

Why is help needed? To mature, a person cannot survive on milk alone. An adult's healthy diet must include protein, whole grains, vegetables and fruit.

Nor can a Christian survive on milk alone. But doesn't the Bible talk about "the milk of the Word"? Yes, it does. Here's what the Apostle Peter wrote:

> Like newborn babies, long for the pure milk of the word, so
> that by it you may grow in respect to salvation.[1]

Doesn't Peter commend the value of milk, that is, the Word? Yes, he does. He tells us to long for it or as some translations have it, "crave" it! But did you notice that Peter addressed his exhortation to newborn babes? Milk is appropriate for babies. Now see what the writer of the book of Hebrews says about milk:

> For everyone who partakes only of milk is not accustomed
> to the word of righteousness, for he is an infant.[2]

The New Living Translation puts it this way: "Someone who partakes only of milk does not know how to do what is right." That's serious stuff! Look at Hebrews where the context, clarifies the issue. The writer, expressing disappointment about the lack of growth in the Hebrew Christians, writes:

> Concerning him [Melchizedek] we have much to say, and it
> is hard to explain, since you have become dull of hearing. For
> though by this time you ought to be teachers, you have need
> again for someone to teach you the elementary principles of
> the oracles of God, and you have come to need milk and
> not solid food.[3]

He is saying that these Christians should have moved on to solid food but they seem *not* to have mastered the fundaments of the faith. In that case, he sadly reports they still need milk. They are not ready for the "meat and potatoes" of the Word. This book will show that solid foods have not been the diet of many contemporary Christians for a long time and many Christians "have need again for someone to teach [them] the elementary principles of the oracles of God." They still need baby bottles!

Apparently, many young people, even those brought up in an evangelical Christian home, are not comfortable with their parents' faith and are not following it. They are leaving their parents' faith by multiple numbers, stunning their parents and disappointing them. However, we will see that

---

[1] 1 Peter 2:2
[2] Hebrews 5:13
[3] Hebrews 5:12

parents often lack convictions about the faith they profess and what faith they do have they project in negative terms. Their children know more about "Thou shalt not!" than they do about "Thou shalt!"

According to George Barna, a Christian pollster, Christians are not doing well in our contemporary culture. What he found is appalling. He put it bluntly in his Annual Report for 2005: "American Christians are biblically illiterate. And the trend line is frightening: the younger a person is, the less they understand about the Christian faith." He says in his 2013 report that the situation shows no improvement. How incongruent! Christians don't know who Christ is! Nor can Christians explain the marvelous thing that has happened to them when they were born again. Nor can they explain what God expects of them to do next!

Barna reports that 40% of Americans claim to be "Christian" but in reality they subscribe to only 8% of his nine points of evangelicalism.[4] These nine points are outlined in his survey report entitled, "Survey Explores Who Qualifies as an Evangelical".

In a blog dated October 14, 2005, Albert Mohler, president of the Southern Baptist Convention, wrote[5] that he was appalled by a comment that researchers George Gallup and Jim Castelli wrote in *The People's Religion: American Faith in the 90's*. They wrote, "Americans revere the Bible—but, by and large, they don't read it. And because they don't read it, they have become a nation of biblical illiterates." [6]

In *Authenticating Your Faith*, you will discover how the advent of television and the repeal of the Sunday Blue Laws[7] have contributed to this frightening issue.

What an astounding and tragic discovery! How can this be and church leadership not be aware of it? If they are aware of it, how is it that little to nothing has been done to counteract it successfully when Barna called it to our attention a decade ago? Christians everywhere, and especially church leaders, should read this and weep! Jesus wondered:

---

[4] Barna reported that respondents were *not* asked to describe themselves as "evangelical."

[5] Mohler, A. (29 June, 2004). *The Scandal of Biblical Illiteracy: It's Our Problem.* http://www.albertmohler.com

[6] George Gallup, Jim Castelli, The People's Religion: American Faith in the 90's, Publisher: Macmillan, 1989

[7] A state or local law that prohibits commercial activities on Sunday

When the Son of Man comes, will He find faith on the earth?[8]

God gave Israel a warning through the prophet Hosea: "My people are destroyed for lack of knowledge".[9]

The institutional church is being destroyed for the same reason and the good life has rendered faith weak. The Church over which Jesus is King is losing its power and influence in America.

Authenticating Your Faith will provide a solid foundation for the faith of any Christian who wants to discover what the Bible really says. Hopefully, it will increase hunger for more of the "meat and potatoes" of the Word. Launch into the study and see how much you know—or how much you don't know.

Anyone who learns to apply biblical truth will experience a metamorphosis into a holy life, from regeneration (having been born again) to sanctification (the process of becoming holy), from a babe in Christ to a maturing holy Christian adult whose thoughts and behavior reflect Christ. The maturing Christian gladly leaves the baby bottle and enjoys the solid food the Lord has prepared. This is sanctification or holiness and sanctification is the Christian's calling:

For God did not call us to be impure, but to live a holy life.[10]

Christians who are tired of the baby bottle and are hungry for solid food will find ample to satisfy that hunger in this study. They will also find many reasons to bless the Lord as they begin to experience the deep spiritual insights God has prepared for His children.[11] Guaranteed!

But the baby bottle must be laid aside first. It provided sustenance for the first period of a Christian's life, but there is so much more in the Word of God waiting for every Christian to "taste and see that that the Lord is good."[12]

The diligent student of the Word will find something else to be true: to learn something new will bless you and immediately create a desire within to share it. Suddenly, the disciple becomes a teacher! The writer of the book of Hebrews would be pleased and so will you and the Lord.

---

[8] Luke 18:8, see also Isaiah 5:12-13
[9] Hosea 4:6
[10] 1 Thessalonians 4:7
[11] 1 Corinthians 2:9-10
[12] Psalm 34:8

VITALS REPORT
A Cause for Concern

I

Vitals are barely responsive; the heart rate is falling! The prognosis? The patient appears to be terminal. She was alive and well, responsive and productive, but now is dying!

Something has happened to the church over the last sixty years leaving many older evangelicals scratching their heads. As noted in the Preface, the Barna Report reveals that Christian illiteracy has increased to the point that Barna simply says, "Christians are biblically illiterate." He reported again in 2013 and said there was no change. The evangelical community seems powerless to reverse the trend, despite the fact that the Lord Jesus said His disciples would go forth proclaiming the Word and signs would follow.[13]

American evangelical churches have made themselves comfortable with the notion that there are no "signs following" because their leaders teach them signs ceased with the death of the Apostles. Where we lived in Africa, Christians witnessed the power of Christ confirming the proclamation of the Gospel. Christians in America wonder why international workers report miracles occurring in other lands, but they do not see them in America.

Sadly, the state of the church in America seems to approximate the church in Laodicea described by the Apostle John in the book of Revelation.[14] What is causing this alarming finding?

---

[13] Matthew 16:20
[14] Revelation 3:14-18

For one thing, boomers and their children are comfortable in a world that values feeling rather than thinking. Therefore, they expect more highly charged emotional gatherings. Sunday morning services now have feel-good messages that stimulate the emotions rather than work with the Holy Spirit to challenge the mind about sin, righteousness, and judgment.[15] For example, hymns that appeal to both the heart and mind have been replaced by choruses that appeal primarily to emotion. These choruses, which contain repeated words with obscure meaning and loud accompaniments, invoke emotions and feelings rather than helping to engage the mind.

John the Baptist's message needs to come through loud and clear, "Repent!"[16] According to Matthew four, Jesus left Nazareth and settled in Capernaum and these words follow: "From that time Jesus began to preach and say, 'Repent, for the kingdom of heaven is at hand.'" Where do we hear the call to repent these days? Are Christians already perfect and therefore do not need to repent of anything?

The new repertoire of music in worship services that appeals to the emotions is supported by many church leaders. "It is the only way to attract the younger people," say the Boomers. (Boomers are those born between 1945-1964.) The result is an increasing number of Boomers in the services and diminishing number of Builders (those born prior to 1945) who do not like the changes. One way of keeping both groups happy is to offer both contemporary and traditional services. Give the Builders what they want! Give the Boomers what they want! Another resolution to the problem that some churches have tried is to offer separate services, the traditional service (for Builders) and the contemporary service (for Boomers). But never the twain shall meet!

Now we have a new generation called the Millennials who have not been exposed to the great hymns of the church, hymns that teach and appeal to the mind, hymns that comfort and convict.

The greatest conundrum of all is this: whatever happened to the Sunday evening evangelistic service for which the Builders have warm memories? Why did it die? Joel Camiskey, president and founder of Joel Comiskey Group, a resource ministry for the worldwide cell church movement, offered this answer:

---

[15] John 16:8
[16] Mark 1:14

Many remember a time in North America when the Sunday evening church service was labeled "evangelism night." Many were won to Christ through those services. Few such services exist today. Most churches have discontinued the Sunday evening services for lack of attendance. The North American, post-Christian culture no longer feels obligated to go to church—whether it's church on Sunday morning or evening.

Now it's time for the church to go to them. The church must move from being the inviting church to becoming the invading church. Gibbs says, "It is commendable for the church to be 'seeker-sensitive' …but now, the church must itself become the seeker. More often than not, they [those being sought] will first need to be befriended by a Christian and linked to a small group of believers who can demonstrate the benefits and challenges of following Christ."[17]

The decline in attendance may also be explained by significant changes in the American culture, including the feminist movement, the youth revolution, and the sexual revolution promoted by the hippies. Add to this, the Vietnam War and the expansion of that war by President Johnson (1963-1969), the civil rights movement and assassination of Martin Luther King (1968), and the Woodstock Musical Festival (1969). These events were turbulent and unsettling, resulting in—and this is extremely important to remember—a societal shift from rationally-based decision-making to emotionally-based decision-making which reflected the values of the hippies.[18]

The arts (including music) reflect these changes as pointed out in *Sing a New Song, When Music Divides the Church.*[19] "Artists wanted to inspire the viewer to leap into the unknown and experience art in their own way."[20] The age of the emphasis on the group (nation, community, church and family) as more important than the individual was over and the exaltation of the individual was introduced, successfully replacing the importance of the group.

---

[17] http://joelcomiskeygroup.com/articles/evangelism/takingchurchtopeople.htm
[18] By this author, published in 1997, and now available only from the author. Contact: bethanyjmr@aol.com
[19] Ibid.
[20] American Culture History, 1960-69, Kingwood College Library, article on the 1960s written by Susan Goodwin and Beck Bradley

Following an absence from the American culture from 1950 through 1967, I returned to the United States to pastor a church and serve the body of local believers. I also enrolled in a sociology program at The University of Toledo to further my education and gain a better understanding of the bewildering changes that had occurred while I was away, particularly in the music field. To say that I was experiencing reverse culture shock immediately after reentry is to put it mildly! I began wondering whether this new music style called rock and roll would eventually find its way into the church. I was aware that jazz music, which had been around since the 1920s, had not impacted church music up to that point.

The Sociology Department, in conjunction with the Music Department, at the University of Toledo permitted me to research the rock musical style and the values of the hippies. My master's thesis was entitled "Musical Taste and Social Experience: An Examination of Factors Related to the Enjoyment of Hard Rock and Heavy Classical Music among Students". It was then, in the 1970s, that I became convinced that the American society was clearly moving philosophically from a rational (thinking) culture, where reason was a priority and emotions were to be kept tightly under control, to the hippies' emotional culture where feeling was valued over reason. At that time, "Let it all hang out" was the motto to live by and "All You Need Is Love, Love, Love" was the theme song. Since it was a developing powerful movement that appealed to young people, would this eventually affect the church? As the years began to pass since my research that is precisely what has happened.

The church has tried to cope with these changes by developing new approaches such as the seeker sensitive movement, the ecumenical movement, the emerging church movement, the house church movement, the charismatic movement, the Christian anarchism movement (rejects the *church*, state or any power other than God), and many self-help books.

Americans, especially younger people who have been brought up on rock and roll, have been flocking to seeker-sensitive churches, which present music using the rock or rock-like musical style. These churches tend to use other emotionally stimulating art including drama and clips from television programs. Willow Creek, the leader in the seeker-sensitive movement, reports they use, "polished music, multimedia, and sermons referencing popular culture and other familiar themes."[21]

---

[21] Branaugh, M. (2008). Willow Creek's "Huge Shift". *Christianity Today.* Retrieved from http://www.christianitytoday.com/ct/2008/june/5.13.html

As indicated in the Preface, the Barna Research Group speaks of the terrible state of Christians, calling them "biblically illiterate." The Sunday morning service, which previously focused on the edification of believers, has been replaced by a focus on evangelism. Because most evangelistic services focus on the salvation of unbelievers; maturing believers do not receive the "meat and potatoes" required to develop and strengthen their faith. To their credit, Willow Creek sensed the need to address this situation (see gray box).

> ### *Influential Megachurch Moves Away from Seeker-Sensitive Services*
>
> After modeling a seeker-sensitive approach to church growth for three decades, Willow Creek Community Church now plans to gear its weekend services toward mature believers seeking to grow in their faith. The change comes on the heels of an ongoing four-year research effort first made public late last summer in Reveal Where Are You? a book coauthored by executive pastor Greg Hawkins. Hawkins said during an annual student ministries conference in April that Willow Creek would also replace its midweek services with classes on theology and the Bible. [22]

While on furlough from Burkina Faso (formerly, Upper Volta) in 1955, 1960, and 1966, I was assigned a schedule of churches to visit and report on my work as a missionary. The schedule indicated I was to stay two or three nights in the homes of church members where I would occasionally hear the strange remark, "We love our pastor, but we don't know what he is talking about!" They could not tell me why the preaching did not meet their needs nor did I question them, not wanting to get involved in local church business beyond the missions program. I was puzzled. Was he not sufficiently trained? Was he preaching over their heads? Was his preaching just theoretical without any practical applications?

Now we have the George Barna Research Group and the Willow Creek staff saying there is a need to return to teaching "theology and the Bible." They found those who described themselves as Christ-centered also said of

---

[22] Ibid.

themselves, they were spiritually stalled or dissatisfied with the role of the church in their spiritual growth. The research goes on to say, "…about a quarter of the 'stalled' segment and 63 percent of the 'dissatisfied' segment contemplated leaving the church." Congregational members were puzzled and many pastors as well.

I found a clue in Dr. Richard Halverson's book with the intriguing title, *How I Changed My Thinking about the Church*. Halverson (1916-1995) served Presbyterian churches in Hollywood, California, and Bethesda, Maryland, and was chaplain of the United States Senate until his death. He authored more than a dozen books and wrote an Introduction for *My Utmost for His Highest* by Oswald Chambers. He also wrote a helpful single page monthly newsletter that found its way into many pastors' mailboxes in the 1970s including mine. I remember him best for a profound encapsulation of biblical truth and the key to my puzzlement.

This is the clue I found. He wrote, "The church gathers for edification and scatters for evangelism." This gathering of the assembly of believers is what defines the church. This truth shaped my philosophy of the church and, for many years, I used this statement on the cover of our church's Sunday bulletin.

"Gathering and scattering" was the practice of the early church although the Jerusalem church did not realize the seriousness of the scattering part until the death of Stephen (Acts 7 and 8). At that time, they were forced out of Jerusalem and *"went everywhere preaching the Gospel."* Believers had remained in Jerusalem for the solid teaching of the Apostles. That was great! They were comfortable and sat tight. But there was the scattering of the Great Commission they were not addressing.[23]

Contemporary Sunday morning services in the seeker service movement are not the meeting of "the church" but an evangelistic rally held in a building that is labeled "church." That in itself is confusing to the unbelievers; meeting in a building called "church," they could say to a friend, "Yes, I went to church last Sunday." This is in line with Webster's definition of the church, which is defined as a building. But Christians need to separate themselves from Webster's definition and return to the biblical definition of "church" as an assembly of believers.

Old-timer evangelicals were scandalized when the Sunday evening evangelistic service ceased to exist. Many churches refused to close down on

---

[23] Matthew 28:19-20

Sunday evenings because, as some felt, they would be like liberal churches which began discontinuing their Sunday evening services decades earlier. Some believed it was the pastor's fault that the unsaved were not making their way to the altar and doubted the effectiveness of the pastor. Pastors felt the congregational members were derelict in their duty to bring in the lost.

Look at the pastor's role and how it is understood today. His role, according to the meaning of the New Testament term is "to feed the flock" (1 Peter 5:2), and it is coupled with the term teacher in Ephesians 4:11. His role is 'pastor-teacher' not 'pastor-evangelist,' but he is forced into the role of evangelist by the leadership who hired him and congregations who have not been properly taught. The church had a Sunday morning service of worship and instruction for believers and an evening 'evangelistic service' to minister to unbelievers. But the pastor-teacher was expected to both instruct the believers and be the evangelist to reach unbelievers.

II

The church has sustained three serious blows as a result of shifts in culture.

The first blow inflicted was the hippies' philosophy that emotions and feelings were valued more than thinking, reasoning, and logic. These latter values are the basis of science and technology that took us right to the atomic bomb—a scary development having power to wipe nations off the face of the earth. But with pressure from the American culture, the church began to adopt a new philosophy about worship that encouraged the uninhibited expression of emotions. This philosophy was embraced without an examination of the "what and why" of the change.

The traditional church saw emotions as out of place in worship services and as a result services became "cut and dried," sterile, and boring. The new philosophy rejects the notion that public gatherings, including the church, have to check their emotions at the door, believing the expression of feelings gives the services more life. Services move along with shouts of "Hallelujah" and speaking in what is assumed to be the biblical gift of tongues.

The second blow was the repeal of the Sunday Blue Laws in many jurisdictions. Laband and Heinbuch wrote:

> Sunday closing laws, or Blue Laws, have a long history.
> In the United States, Blue Laws date back to the colonial

times. Across the ocean, restrictions on Sunday activities go back to the days of the Roman Empire under the Emperor Constantine. A discussion of Sunday closing Blue Laws isn't just history because the policy debate over Sunday closings has a way of periodically springing up, first in one community, then in another, followed by yet another.[24]

The third blow to the church was the availability of affordable television sets and the prime time programming that soon developed. When the Sunday closing laws were in effect, the only gig in town (to borrow a contemporary expression) was the evangelical Sunday evening service. For believers, Sunday was revered as the Sabbath, a day to attend church services and worship God. However, for many unbelievers, this day brought boredom and frustration. To address this, the Sunday evening church service offered unbelievers an opportunity to attend a less formal and less liturgical program that focused more on music.

Prime time television pre-empted all of that when sports were scheduled for Sunday afternoon and Sunday evening. Now there were many exciting gigs in town from an unbeliever's point of view. When remotes became available, those who stayed home, weren't even obliged to get out of their La-Z-Boys except to raid the refrigerator for a snack or to use the bathroom during commercials!

But there are problems in the church, too. The church, following cultural trends and trying to compete with secular programming on TV, has failed miserably. The cost is one problem and moral failures another. Unless churches had lots of money to spend on advertising, they had to settle for the mediocre. Mediocre soon became boring for the Boomers.

Believers developed the habit of going to church regularly and remained faithful to Sunday services, morning and evening. If they missed attending those services, they would report their week was all messed up!

George Barna in his book entitled, *Revolution*, published in 2005, tells of a new revolution sweeping the land. Unlike The Great Awakening when new believers were swept into the church, this contemporary revolution is sweeping them out of the church. Well, maybe not exactly. As we have seen above, they are not being fed, and have no reason to stay in their churches. This new

---

[24] "Blue Laws, The History, Economics, and Politics of Sunday-Closing Laws" by David N. Laband and Deborah Hendry Heinbuch (s1987, 2008), D. C. Heath and Company.

revolution gives them reason for leaving. In an article printed by *Christianity Today* entitled, "No Church, No Problem," the opening line is this, "George Barna wants commitment to the local congregation to sink lower than ever." The reviewer, Kevin Miller tells about Barna's view of baptisms, marriages, and the sacraments:

> That's only a "congregational-formatted ministry," one of many ways to "develop and live a faith-centered life. We made it up." Writes Barna, "Whether you become a revolutionary immersed in, minimally involved in, or completely disassociated from a local church is irrelevant to me (and, within boundaries, to God)… My goal is to help you be a revolutionary."[25]

In the review, Miller tells of Barna's fictional character who illustrates what I just pointed out: people are bored in churches because church leadership is missing the importance of the "meat and potatoes" of the Word. It is the Word that provides stimulation of the soul and spirit. Here is more of Miller's review:

> Barna illustrates with two fictional characters who "eliminated church life from their busy schedules." Why? They did not find a ministry "that was sufficiently stimulating" and "their church, although better than average, still seems flat."

Miller concluded his review by explaining that the original Reformers pointed to the importance of the local church. He said:

> They insisted that every believer be immersed in a local congregation, where the gospel is rightly proclaimed and the sacraments rightly administered. The notion of freelance Christians would have made them spit out their beer. Miller identified the need for church services where the gospel is rightly proclaimed.

The gospel is much more than preaching the necessity for the new birth. The starting point is indeed regeneration, but there is also sanctification and glorification. Salvation is all three and this book, *Authenticate Your Faith, Here's How and Why*, explains the full plan of salvation which is the magnificent and complete gospel that Jesus came to validate by His death

---

[25] http://www.christianitytoday.com/ct/2006/january/13.69.html

and resurrection. This is what He commanded His followers to proclaim in all the world.

Nearly five decades ago, A. W. Tozer identified and explained the same need in his book, *Man: the Dwelling Place of God*. In his usual style, he clearly and succinctly presented the reason why the church has become powerless, an anathema to so many church members, and a laugh to many unbelievers. Tozer wrote:

> Christianity today is man-centered, not God-centered. God is made to wait patiently, even respectfully, on the whims of men. The image of God currently popular is that of a distracted Father, struggling in heartbroken desperation to get people to accept a Savior of whom they feel no need and in whom they have very little interest. To persuade these self-sufficient souls to respond to His generous offers God will do almost anything, even using salesmanship methods and talking down to them in the chummiest way imaginable. This view of things is, of course, a kind of religious romanticism which, while it often uses flattering and sometimes embarrassing terms in praise of God, manages nevertheless to make man the star of the show.[26]

In a report by George Barna, "The Bible in America 2013," one section is entitled, "What do Americans really think of the Bible?" David Kinnaman, president of the Barna Group, points to several conclusions from the study; here is the first of his four conclusions:

> Most Americans esteem the Bible and have access to it. However, even if there's a baseline of respect, people aren't sure how to apply the lessons of Scripture to public life or society, particularly in an increasingly pluralistic nation.

That's the job of pastor-teachers! But teaching a congregation how to apply scriptural truths is evidently not taking place as it ought to. *Authenticate Your Faith* was written to address these issues, first as scripts for a radio program called "In the Classroom," and then as a basis for this book.

When church members fail to see God at work in their church family or in their personal lives, they have no reason to stay. If they choose to stay

---

[26] Tozer, A. W. (2008). *Man the Dwelling Place of God: What it Means to Have Christ Living in You*. Moody Press

in that setting, they quit being *theists* and become *deists*. Deists believe in a creator God who quit taking an active part in the life of their church and placed the running of the world in man's hands. Works, such as praying, tithing, singing songs and attendance have become necessary to gain God's approval. Emotional expressions have substituted for the engagement of the mind. Spiritual worship remains elusive.

This book addresses biblical concepts that are poorly understood by the average Christian today. Failing to grasp these strategic concepts will leave one with tunnel vision and both a distorted view of the gospel and a lack of personal holiness that Christians must have if they are to see God.

> Therefore, "come out from their midst
> and be separate," says the Lord,
> "and do not touch what is unclean;
> And I will welcome you,
> And I will be a father to you,
> And you shall be sons and daughters
> to Me," Says the Lord Almighty.
> ***
> Therefore, having these promises,
> beloved, let us cleanse ourselves
> from all defilement of flesh and spirit
> perfecting holiness in the fear of God.
> ***
> Like the Holy One who called you,
> be holy yourselves also in all your
> behavior; because it is written,
> "You shall be holy, for I am holy."

CHAPTER 1

INTRODUCING
THE MAN FROM NAZARETH
AKA PODUNK

I

How much do you know about Nazareth? Did you know the Jewish leaders in Jesus' day viewed Nazareth as Podunk? True, two thousand years ago, they didn't know the word Podunk, but the references to Nazareth in Scripture smack of Podunk.

Is there really such a place as Podunk? Not in Israel, but there are several Podunk towns in the United States. So why Podunk when thinking of Nazareth? Why would Jerusalem leadership put Nazareth in the same category as Podunk? What does Podunk mean? What's its origin?

In 1869, Mark Twain popularized the word Podunk when he defended the Rev. Thomas Beecher, a friend whose preaching had stirred up controversy. In an article of about 1800 words titled, "Mr. Beecher and the Clergy," he wrote in reference to the controversy and concluded, "They even know it in Podunk, wherever that may be."

For the record, the word Podunk is of Algonquian origin denoting the Podunk people who occupied a territory that is now southern New England.[1] The word probably meant "marshy areas." A search will show there is a Podunk in Vermont, Pennsylvania, Michigan, Indiana, and elsewhere.

---

[1] "Podunk". Wikipedia Free Encyclopedia. Retrieved from https://en.wikipedia.org/wiki/Podunk

Its use in American English is explained this way: "It has come to denote a place of small size or 'in the middle of nowhere,' and is often used, upper-cased, as a name in a context of dismissing significance or importance."[2]

That was exactly the attitude of the leadership in Jerusalem about Galilee, the province where Nazareth was (and is) located. This Northern Province was filling up with Gentiles from countries north and east. In addition, the leadership could find no Old Testament reference to Nazareth or any prophecy about their Messiah coming from Nazareth. To them, it was pure Podunk and "unclean" because of the Gentile influx. Would an orthodox Jew go to Galilee? No! How then could a Messiah come from Podunk?

The inhabitants in neighboring towns in Galilee didn't think very much of Nazareth either. Nothing of a religious nature could be connected with Nazareth, they thought, as the interchange between Philip of Bethsaida (located in Galilee) and Nathaniel, also of Bethsaida, reveals. When he responded to Philip, Nathaniel was no doubt reflecting what their hometown thought of Nazareth, a distance of thirty miles away as the crow flies (but longer if traveling the path that Jesus walked in His day). Here is their conversation.

> Philip found Nathaniel and said to him, "We have found Him of whom Moses in the Law and also the Prophets wrote—Jesus of Nazareth, the son of Joseph." Nathaniel said to him, "Can any good thing come out of Nazareth?" Philip said to him, "Come and see."[3]

We are told:

> A special contempt seemed to rest upon [Nazareth] over and above the general contempt in which all Galilee was held, from the number of Gentiles that settled in the upper territories of it, and, in the estimation of the Jews, [it was] debased. Thus, in the providential arrangement by which our Lord was brought up at the insignificant and

---

[2] "Podunk". Merriam-Webster Online. Retrieved from http://www.merriam-webster.com/dictionary/Podunk

[3] John 1:45-46

opprobrious[4] town called Nazareth, there was involved…a local humiliation.[5]

After Herod died, it was safer for Joseph to return from Egypt and take his family straight to Nazareth, bypassing Bethlehem, a town located a half-dozen miles from Jerusalem. No doubt they had relatives in Bethlehem since Mary and Joseph were both of the lineage of David. Bethlehem was their hometown and apparently it was not safe for them to live there. Neither was it safe for their relatives or for the shepherds who had witnessed the angels singing. After paying a visit to the newborn baby in the stable, they went everywhere proclaiming what they had seen.

II

Matthew says the Messiah is called a "Nazarene," apparently a vague reference to Isaiah 11:1 in the Old Testament. From that passage, Matthew connects the words twig and Nazareth. The Matthew passage reads:

> But when he heard that Archelaus was reigning over Judea in place of his father Herod, he was afraid to go there. Then after being warned by God in a dream, he left for the regions of Galilee, and came and lived in a city called Nazareth. This was to fulfill what was spoken through the prophets: "He shall be called a Nazarene."[6]

It would appear the Gospel writer is reaching a bit; however, it is generally accepted that he wrote under the inspiration of the Holy Spirit. Theologians are divided as to whether or not Matthew had Isaiah 11:1 in mind. That reference reads:

> Then a shoot will spring from the stem of Jesse,
>
> And a branch from his roots will bear fruit.[7]

---

[4] Meaning, "deserving of scorn, contempt, or severe criticism"

[5] Jamieson, R., Brown, D., and Fausset, A. (1872).*A Commentary, Critical, Experimental, and Practical, on the Old and New Testaments* (5), p.10. William Collins.

[6] Matthew 2:23

[7] The New International Version

The Jewish leadership understood this text to refer to the Messiah. Matthew also understood this text to be Messianic; but how did he make the connection with Nazareth and get the word "Nazarene" from that Hebrew text? Since Hebrew is written using only consonants, Matthew saw the similarity of the consonants in the word Nazareth, n-z-r, and the identical consonants in the Hebrew word "branch/twig," n-z-r. There are two meanings for the consonants n-z-r. The primary meaning is "the guarded one" or "fortress" and a secondary meaning is "shoot," as in sprout, sucker, or twig. Matthew, under the inspiration of the Holy Spirit, saw a third meaning for n-z-r, "Nazareth."

Their scholars knew the Messiah was to come from Judah. They were correct when they read in the Old Testament the Messiah was to be born in Bethlehem.[8] Nazareth was Podunk, a place not worth talking about. However, Nazareth is important to Christians because that is where Jesus spent about thirty of His thirty-three years.

Since the Jerusalem leaders came to the conclusion—erroneously—that Jesus was born in Nazareth, Galilee, they dismissed Him altogether! They put the burden of proof on Jesus to prove He was from God, but they had no expectation that He could be their Messiah.

The important question was not "Where did you come from?" in order to draw conclusions as to whether or not he should be given a hearing. Rather, they should have asked "What does this person, Jesus, have to say that will make a positive contribution to our lives, have we vetted this person adequately, and do we know all the facts?"

III

Why is Podunk important to Jesus and our salvation? Since the Jerusalem leaders viewed Jesus as "a nobody from Podunk", it meant Jesus had to work hard with wisdom and humility to overcome that false assumption and in the process fulfill prophecy. In the synagogue at Nazareth, Jesus quoted Isaiah's prophecy that explained who He really was.[9] Here is what Jesus said:

---

[8] Micah 5:2
[9] Isaiah 61:1-2a, quoted by Luke in Chapter 4:18-19

> The Spirit of the Lord God is upon me,
> the Lord has anointed me to bring good news to the afflicted;
> He has sent me to bind up the brokenhearted, to
> proclaim liberty to captives and freedom to prisoners;
> To proclaim the favorable year of the Lord...

Jesus did not add the next two lines found in Isaiah's prophecy since He had come the first time to offer salvation, not mete out condemnation. The Day of Vengeance will occur at His Second Advent. The words, "the favorable year of the Lord" referred to His first coming.

Here are those two lines—well known surely by those in the synagogue who may have thought He was talking about taking vengeance on them instead of the Romans. Here is what Jesus did not add:

> ...and the day of vengeance of our God; To comfort all who mourn.

They would not listen to what He did say justifying His right to preach. They angrily drove Him out of the synagogue intent on doing Him bodily harm.

Had He made His true identity clear by fireworks and thunderbolts (He could have, you know), the leaders would have thrown Him in prison early and cut His ministry short. He could have taken two of them and knocked their heads together for not listening when He said, "He who has ears to hear let him hear." He didn't do that because His message was one of love, grace, and mercy.

Can you imagine what was going on in the heads of those leaders? "He acts like a Messiah, but that 'Nazareth connection'...! That surely eliminates Him. He's an imposter! There have been many false prophets, and He is one of them!" Did the leadership understand who He was claiming to be? Yes, they really did and decided to kill Him because of His claim. To them, His claim was utter blasphemy. "But He is an itinerant preacher, a bumpkin from Podunk. We'll let Him be for the time being, but if the crowds begin to follow him—then we'll kill Him."

> For this reason therefore the Jews were seeking all the more
> to kill Him, because He not only was breaking the Sabbath,

but also was calling God His own Father, making Himself equal with God.[10]

At that point they would have ample opportunity to accept Him as their Lord and Savior or reject Him. Rejecting Him would seal their fate. Their judgment would be substantial because they were also guilty of mistreating strangers, widows, and orphans for whom God has a special affinity.[11]

Isaiah foresaw the difficult road the Messiah would travel and the cruel treatment He would receive before men and women would recognize Him as the Son of God and the Savior of the world. Isaiah prophesied about the Messiah's rejection and extreme suffering:

> He was despised and forsaken of men, a man of sorrows and acquainted with grief… Surely our griefs He Himself bore, and our sorrows He carried. But He was pierced through for our transgressions, He was crushed for our iniquities; the chastening for our well-being fell upon Him, and by His scourging we are healed.[12]

Jesus knew what Isaiah had written about Him but, despite what lay before Him, Jesus invited those for whom He was about to die to come to Him and find rest.

> Come to Me, all who are weary and heavy-laden, and I will give you rest. Take My yoke upon you and learn from Me, for I am gentle and humble in heart[13] and you will find rest for your souls.[14] For My yoke is easy and My burden is light.[15]

IV

Moses and Elijah, who appeared with Jesus on the Mount of Transfiguration, were also men of humble beginnings.

Moses' Podunk was called Goshen, an area located in the eastern Delta of the Nile. After Jacob moved to Egypt at his son Joseph's invitation, he and

---

[10] John 5:18
[11] Exodus 22:22; Deuteronomy 10:18-19; Zechariah 7:10; Matthew 23:14; Mark 12:38:40
[12] Isaiah 53:3a, 4a, 5
[13] Zechariah 9:9
[14] Jeremiah 6:16
[15] Matthew 11:28-29, cf. Ezekiel 34:27

his family were given the land of Goshen. It was home to the Israelites for four hundred years. When a new Pharaoh rose to power who did not know Joseph, he enslaved the Israelites and decreed that all baby boys be put to death in order to control the growth of the Israelite population. To protect Moses, his mother and father devised a plan to hide their son and save him from the Pharaoh's decree. Their baby boy's first public appearance was in a basket floating on the river among the reeds, while his sister watched over him.

Pharaoh's daughter found him there, retrieved him from the basket, adopted him, and called him Moses; he grew to adulthood in Pharaoh's palace. He ventured out one day and saw an Egyptian abusing an Israelite. He injected himself into the fray and killed the Egyptian. Immediately, Moses fled to the Midian wilderness—*where?* Yes, call it Podunk. Goshen and the Midian wilderness were geographical regions. What town or city did Moses say he was from? We are not told.

Moses became Israel's leader and served for forty years. Not bad for a man whose folks lived in Goshen (Podunk) and for a man who lived in the desert with distant relatives,[16] the Midianites (another Podunk).

Speaking of Podunk, Gilead could also be called Podunk. And guess who came from this Podunk? Elijah. He was called a "sojourner in Gilead" meaning he was not a native-born son of Gilead, the name of a city and a region located on the east side of the Jordan River.[17] So where did his family really come from? We are not told. His father's name is not given so the family may have been Gentiles who had immigrated to Gilead from somewhere else and adopted Israel's God.

Years before, when Joseph was held prisoner by his brothers in a cistern, he was pulled out and sold to merchants traveling to Egypt; the Scriptures identify those merchants as Ishmaelites from Gilead.[18] This territory was awarded to the half tribe of Manasseh.

Many expositors of the Old Testament agree that the word used in 1 Kings 17:1 referring to Elijah means a "sojourner". It is translated elsewhere as foreigner. Hebrew scholar, Gesenius,[19] defines the Hebrew word *towshab*

---

[16] Genesis 25:1-2, the Midianites claimed Abraham as their ancestor since Midian was a son of Abraham (his mother was Keturah whom Abraham married after Sarah died); Moses traced his lineage back to Levi, a great-grandson of Abraham

[17] 1 Kings 17:1. Holman Christian Standard Bible (HCSB) translates the phrase: "from the Gilead settlers"

[18] Genesis 37:25

[19] Gesenius' Hebrew-Chaldee Lexicon to the Old Testament Scriptures (1846)

as "a stranger, an emigrant, sojourning in a strange country, where he is not naturalized." It would seem, therefore, that his parents were proselytes to Judaism because they gave their baby boy a God-honoring Hebrew name, "My-God-Is-Yah" (Yah stands for Jehovah or Yahweh). We know him as Elijah.

Jewish commentators see Elijah as the greatest of all prophets and cannot believe that Elijah might have been a Gentile. They offer several reasons to support their argument, but they appear to be mostly speculative. When I think of the possibility of Elijah representing the Gentiles on the Mount of Transfiguration and Moses representing the Jews, both sitting there with Jesus, I have goose bumps!

Moses and Elijah were both bold and courageous prophets for God. A millennium apart, both men went before a king, dressed like peasants, to deliver a message from God. The messages were delivered unflinchingly and then each left town in a hurry with their respective king chasing after them, trying to capture them and drag them back to the capital city. Did the Father *pick* them to sit on the Mount of Transfiguration with His Son Jesus because of these exploits for which we admire them and call them great?

No, God doesn't pick those to serve Him whom men and women think are great. Rather, He chooses those who will listen to His voice and obey His commands no matter how difficult and dangerous they are. We know Moses objected at first, and I wouldn't be surprised that Elijah also objected at first. But they both fulfilled the mission entrusted to them.

Old Testament leaders were chosen to provide insight into the great Leader-to-come, Jesus Christ, who also came from Podunk. Three years later, He cried out in agony to His Heavenly Father because of the assignment His Father gave Him to do, but He settled the issue with the words, "Not my will but Yours be done."[20]

Moses, arriving from Midian surely evoked laughter from those in Pharaoh's court because of his clothing. We can hear the Pharaoh who did not know Moses, thunder, "Quiet! Who is this peasant and what does he want?"

Elijah, the peasant from Gilead, must have evoked the same laughter in Ahab's court. But the laughter turned to deathly silence when he was introduced and stated the purpose for which he had come. The sergeant-at-arms would have said, "My lord, this is My-God-is-Jehovah." That surely got the king's attention immediately because he and his wife Jezebel assumed they

---

[20] Luke 22:42

had stamped out any mention of Jehovah in Israel. They had ordered all the altars dedicated to Jehovah be torn down. God took note of that and then took action in His time.

Jesus, the country boy from Podunk in Galilee, had to earn the respect of His listeners. He began with a group of twelve disciples around Him—mostly fishermen. He promised them He would make them fishers of men. Since His message was compelling, it was hard to dismiss him and laugh Him off. He was radical! He taught using interesting stories and parables with which the crowd could identify.

At the trial of Jesus, Peter was accused of being from Podunk and having been associated with the now fallen-from-favor Jesus. Peter's dialect gave him away and they asked accusingly, "You are one of them too!" But Peter said, "Man, I am not!"[21]

"On the day of Pentecost, the crowds were amazed to hear the proclamation of the Good News about Jesus Christ in their own languages and made the comment "Are these not all Galileans?"[22] They could tell where the Apostles came from by their dress and, when they spoke to each other, by their dialect. Their question no doubt was a cross between being derisive and amazed. But as they listened, they heard the message of salvation each in his own dialect. The disciples were speaking clearly in the languages of the listeners—dozens of languages according to Acts 2.

Appreciate the fact that the Jewish leaders of Jesus' day were confused by Jesus' dialect and the way He dressed; His mannerisms, dialect, and clothing were all Podunk. There was no question about that! He was a product of His home as all children are.

But their Messiah? They believed their Messiah would appear suddenly riding into Jerusalem not on a young donkey, but on a horse, that He would prove Himself a worthy descendant of King David, and that He would be ready to take on the oppressive rulers of the Roman Empire. Their Messiah would be welcomed as he came brandishing a spear and shield.

That's what the crowds were led to believe by the Jewish leadership. But that is not what the Scriptures taught. Because of the miracles Jesus performed, they were confused.[23] Imagine! In His hands, a boy's lunch became enough for thousands! A man dead for four days, came out of the tomb! Yes, He could

---

[21] Luke 22:58
[22] Acts 2:7
[23] John 7:27, 41

be the Messiah. Maybe—or maybe not? Maybe their leaders were wrong—or were they right?

The leaders in Jerusalem were biased in their vetting. The Messiah had to fit their understanding of the Law that, by Jesus' day, had been encrusted with hundreds of man-made regulations. Their bias blinded them to the truth that this Man from Podunk was their Messiah. When they came to the conclusion that He really was saying that God was His Father—and meant it—they began to shut their ears and yell, "Heresy! Heresy!" How could words like that come out of a mere mortal, a man from Podunk at that! They had strong negative feelings.

The Jews answered [Pilate], "We have a law, and by that law He ought to die because He made Himself out to be the Son of God." The "Tourist Israel" website offers this surprising comment about modern Nazareth, calling it, "The Forgotten Son of Israeli tourism [that] not only has over a dozen important Christian sites, but as Israel's largest Arab city, has some fascinating cultural sites and experiences to savor."

Independence, Missouri, had little significance to the rest of America until the haberdasher, Harry S. Truman, became president. Whoever heard of the tiny village in southwest Georgia called Plains until Jimmy Carter became president? The world has come to know Nazareth because it was Jesus' home for thirty years. If Nazareth provoked derisive comments in Jesus' day, it surely does not do so these days.

But, more importantly, today, Nazareth is remembered wherever the Gospel is preached.

V

An important question remains: Why did Jesus have to grow up in Podunk?

First, Podunk humbled anyone who came from Podunk. That included Moses and Elijah, as we have noted, as well as many others in the Old Testament. In the New Testament, look at the hitherto unknown individuals who suddenly appeared on the scene in Luke Chapters 1 and 2: Zacharias (Zechariah) and Elizabeth, Joseph and Mary, and most notably, Jesus. What did they have in common? They are all described as "righteous." The point? The righteous unknowns were humble enough and willing to listen to the voice of God and they saw their lives transformed.

Second, there is an important phrase in Scripture that describes Jesus' time of growing up in Nazareth and preparing for the ultimate sacrifice at Calvary: "Although He was a Son, He learned obedience from the things which He suffered."[24] Some assume that phrase refers only to His treatment at the hands of the Jewish leadership and His final passion. The text does not limit it to that. He had to act and react like a human being and that was altogether new to Jesus just as it is to all children. He "laid aside" His divine nature so as to be fully human.[25] He put His deity on hold.[26]

Third, Jesus had to rely on Joseph to teach him the discipline of carpentry and Mary to show Him the loving relationship of a mother. As He was growing up, Jesus learned about human emotions, how tricky they can be, and how to handle them.

Fourth, Jesus was in the wings for thirty years but Podunk was not a waste of time. Was He tempted to disobey His parents? Sure. "He faced all of the same testings we do, yet he did not sin."[27] Did He ever disobey or have a rebellious spirit? No. That would have been sin. We have a rebellious spirit from our father Adam, but Jesus' Father was God. We will examine that relationship in the next chapter.

As a boy He would have joined the boys of his day to learn reading and writing and to memorize much of the Scriptures (the Old Testament). Later, as He taught the people, He often quoted Scripture.

When Jesus taught, He showed love and compassion for children who were brought to Him. He championed women, especially the woman caught in adultery who was brought to Him. He could also be offended and expressed righteous indignation when He proceeded to overturn the merchants' tables in the temple and thundered "Woe unto you, Pharisees and Scribes." His time with His parents was time well spent. After His baptism in the Jordan River, Jesus relied on the Holy Spirit to show Him the will of His Father God.

A child learns to function as a human being through the love and discipline of parents. The child is taught the traditions and customs of his or her culture. Jesus was no exception. He was once a baby, then a toddler, a youngster, a teenager, and eventually, a well-balanced, mature young man. His small town upbringing (i.e., Podunk) was likely more helpful in bringing about this balance and maturity than Jerusalem would have been.

---

[24] Hebrews 5:8

[25] Philippians 2

[26] Philippians 2:6-8

[27] Hebrews 4:15 (NLT)

Jesus was fully a human being. For example, he learned carpenter skills from Joseph, a skilled carpenter. I can picture Joseph teaching Jesus how to hold a hammer and use an adz correctly. Before going to the mission field, a carpenter in the church where I pastored taught me how to hold a hammer. With the first couple of tries, my mentor said firmly but kindly, "No, not that way. This way." Then I got it and used that skill as I was building our home in West Africa. I'm sure Joseph taught Jesus how to hold a hammer properly.

We sometimes think that when Jesus was on earth, He knew everything and could do everything. We are in error when we take that position. What He said and what He did right were a result of being in subjection to Mary and Joseph, and, when He began His public ministry, His life was in total subjection to the voice of the Holy Spirit who came upon Him at His baptism. He lived as a human being, temporarily laying aside His divine prerogatives.

The Apostle Paul spells that out in Philippians 2, where it is written that He was "in very nature God," but He "made Himself nothing." More precisely, "He emptied Himself" and we can presume that is a reference to the fact that He put His divine nature on hold.

What was Jesus doing in His twenties? We have no record of those years, but can we not suppose He practiced the trade He was taught? He certainly would not have been idle from puberty to age thirty when He began His ministry as an itinerant Teacher.

Artists have painted fanciful and unrealistic pictures of a young Jesus. They forgot He was a child of Podunk with a human mother and foster father and that His family was poor. Yes, He was totally human, experiencing the same temptations and weaknesses and the same emotions as the rest of us experience. The writer of the book of Hebrews wrote:

> During the days of Jesus' life on earth, he offered up prayers and petitions with fervent cries and tears to the one who could save him from death, and he was heard because of his reverent submission. Although He was a Son, He learned obedience from what He suffered.[28]

Fifth, here's another important reason God had Jesus spend thirty years in Podunk. Nazareth obscured the fact that He was born in Bethlehem. And why was that important? His heavenly Father knew His Son needed to learn humility (humility is *learned,* you know) and being from a town that had

---

[28] Hebrews 5:7 (NIV)

an undesirable reputation—who would want to go to Nazareth since there was nothing to see or do there? God selected the town where Jesus could experience a normal childhood. Nazareth was ideal for that purpose.

CHAPTER 2

INTRODUCING
THE MAN FROM HEAVEN
AKA HIS FATHER'S HOUSE

I

The word was buzzed around the West African village of Ouarkoye[1] that the son of God had come to town and that he would speak to the villagers in the morning. He asked for and was given a sumptuous meal and he was showered with gifts. Was this the Son of God the missionaries were talking about? They would find out in the morning.

Morning came and the villagers assembled in front of the hut where this purported son of God was housed for the night. These African houses were constructed of mud brick and had no windows. The door opening was covered over with a woven mat made of tall grass. There were no doors or locks as thieves and robbers were not yet a problem in this bush country; fear of retribution from household fetishes kept them safe.

The villagers rose up early the next morning. Assembling at the door, they discovered there was no noise coming from the hut where the son of God was housed for the night. They waited. The mat still covered the door. They waited some more. After a while the villagers grew restless and then puzzled and a man went to the doorway and clapped several times. Still there was no response. They grew suspicious and eventually someone dared to pull the grass

---

[1] Located in Burkina Faso (formerly Upper Volta). West Africa

15

mat aside and look inside. There was no one there. The self-proclaimed son of God and his gifts were gone. They had been deceived.

In recounting the story to me, a villager said he himself had a small camera—probably the only one in the entire village—but never thought to take a picture. He said he heard the son of God had visited another town several miles away where the townspeople also gave him a great meal and showered him with gifts. He left that village before addressing the villagers also. "Perhaps he was in a hurry to get to our town," he mused. He certainly was!

Most of the villagers in the tribe at that point in time were illiterate, but the fellow giving the report had an elementary school education. He had little or no understanding as to who the real Son of God was. He thought their visitor was displeased with the previous town. Therefore, he hurried on to come and bless them and their town. But he speculated that he must have been displeased with what he found in Ouarkoye as well! Did he not come to give them a special message from the God in heaven about whom they knew so little? He no doubt moved on to the next town, to receive better gifts than they could give, he concluded.

The quickest mode of transportation was one's two feet. As quickly as this false Messiah came, he ate their food, received their gifts, and was gone, leaving under cover of darkness. Where did he go? No one knew; the townspeople were confused and the devil smirked.

Jesus spent most of His life in Podunk, a town of little reputation, and it took Him three years of preaching to convey a message that He was the One who was truly the Son of God and that His Father was God in Heaven. His mode of transportation was His two feet. Nevertheless, He got the message out and they killed Him for this declaration. The proof for every skeptic is His resurrection from the dead.

All others are deceivers and their message is always one of self-enhancement and for selfish gain. Jesus' message was consistent with the prophets in the Old Testament and with the forerunner, John the Baptist. The message was about sin, righteousness, and repentance.

There have been many self-proclaimed sons of God over the ages. Jesus said there would be many[2] but He alone is the true Son of God, anointed to be Savior of the world.

---

[2] Matthew 24

II

A new generation of missionaries went out to West Africa following World War II. They were asked to learn the languages of local tribes. In Burkina Faso (formerly Upper Volta[3]), a country the size of Colorado, there were over seventy tribal languages. We were asked to learn a language called Bobo Oulé (Red Bobo), now called Bwamu. We searched for words that would explain the Gospel message clearly.

It was important to explain to those who gave us a hearing that Jesus did not come for a handout nor does He ever come to our homes to deceive us. He came to serve not to be served.[4] He was God's Son, born in a small town like theirs. He came from Heaven, yes, the place that exceeds the Garden of Eden in beauty. This is the place Jesus referred to when He taught His disciples to pray: "Our Father who is *in heaven*, Hallowed be Your name." Mary's husband, Joseph, was his legal father, but God was His true Father.

The religious leaders knew their Messiah was going to come from the stock of Jesse, King David's father, and therefore would be a "son of David".[5] He would be born in Bethlehem.[6] Apparently they never asked Jesus where He was born. Since He dressed liked those from Galilee and had the Galilee accent,[7] He was Galilean as far as they were concerned. As to His Father, He made it absolutely clear that God was His Father.[8] That was unacceptable to the Jewish leadership.

In the beginning of His ministry, the Pharisees were puzzled about Jesus. They said they knew where He came from, and it certainly was not Heaven! They were certain they knew His father, and He certainly was not God!

> They said, "Is this not Jesus, the son of Joseph, whose father and mother we know? How can he now say, 'I came down from heaven'?"[9]

---

[3] Independence from France came in 1960, the name change followed

[4] Luke 22:27, "For who is greater, the one who reclines at the table or the one who serves? Is it not the one who reclines at the table? But I am among you as the one who serves."

[5] For the Jews the term "son" also means "a descendent"

[6] Micah 5:2

[7] During Jesus' trial, Peter was standing alongside a fire to keep warm and a man looked at him and recognized he was a Galilean according to Luke 22:59

[8] John 5:18

[9] John 6:42

The Pharisees said they knew the Scriptures prophesied a coming Messiah but they were persuaded God was obliged to send them a strong militant Messiah like Joshua to deliver them from the Romans. Jesus' name reminded them of Joshua since Jesus (savior) is Greek for Joshua (savior), the Hebrew form. But, they were also skeptical of this man who was calling Heaven his "Father's House". They knew what they needed and it was not a benevolent Messiah going about doing good! The true Messiah, they believed, would take up a spear and sword and call up the troops.

Jesus healed a man who had been an invalid for thirty-eight years. Then Jesus told him to take up his pallet and carry it home. He did so. The leaders were hard put to understand why Jesus would encourage anyone to take up his bed and carry on the Sabbath. Their Sabbath rules prohibited carrying such things on the Sabbath. This proved that Jesus was a Sabbath-breaker. Certainly if God was His Father, He (God) would not approve of His Son breaking Sabbath laws!

Since Jesus' acts of healing the sick didn't square with the Sabbath laws they had developed, the leadership felt obliged to stop Jesus. They would kill Him if necessary and would believe they were doing God a favor. Jesus offered this response: "My Father is always at His work to this very day, and I, too, am working."

Jesus' statement has two instructive elements. The first is about His Father working "to this very day." The Pharisees, well acquainted with the Scriptures knew that Genesis says God created the world in six days and on the seventh day He rested. They also knew that when God gave Moses the first covenant, its foundation was the Ten Commandments in which this commandment is found: "Remember the Sabbath day to keep it holy." The Scripture goes on to explain, "...the seventh day is a Sabbath of Jehovah, your God."[10] In Hebrew, the word Sabbath means rest.

The Jews developed a network of regulations to make sure the seventh day was preserved as a day of rest from weekly toil. These laws related to cooking, the distance one could walk on the Sabbath, how much one could pick up and carry, and so on. The Talmud tractate *Shabbat*, identifies thirty-nine categories of activity prohibited on the Sabbath.[11] The rabbis would discuss

---

[10] Exodus 20:8-10

[11] "Activities prohibited on *Shabbat*, based on the Mishnah *Shabbat* 7:2"; the first eleven categories are: "1 Planting, 2 Plowing, 3 Reaping, 4 Gathering, 5 Threshing/Extraction, 6 Winnowing, 7 Sorting/Purification, 8 Grinding, 9 Sifting, 10 Kneading, 11 Cooking/Baking" —Wikipedia Free Encyclopedia

difficult questions that arose from time to time, such as: A person can't pick up a stone on the Sabbath, but he or she can pick up a child on the Sabbath. Question: can a person pick up a child who is carrying a stone? They lost sight of the purpose of the Sabbath when they imposed a long list of don'ts.

Not only did they rebuke Jesus for healing on the Sabbath, they rebuked Him because they saw His disciples pluck some grain in a field not yet harvested and it occurred on the Sabbath.[12] The text says they were hungry and plucking some grain was legal, but doing it on the Sabbath was not. "They broke the 'Sabbath' in two respects; to pluck was to reap, and to rub was to thresh."[13] Reaping and threshing on the Sabbath were forbidden. Surely the Son of God would not be engaging in this type of behavior.

Jesus reminded them they could pull a sheep out of a ditch on the Sabbath but were persecuting Him because He healed a man and made him whole on the Sabbath. Jesus clarified what could be done on the Sabbath rather than what must not be done. To the Jewish leadership Jesus said, "How much more valuable is a person than a sheep! Therefore it is lawful to do good on the Sabbath."[14]

Secondly, what was He doing? If He rested on the seventh day, how could He be still working? If their God Jehovah was still working, what was He doing? It's obvious He rested from the work He was doing and that work was creation. It was done, finished, completed! And since the Jews were His chosen people, they could honor Him by resting on the day He rested. God then turned to something else. Something that was foundational to the entire flow of history: saving the human race. He was—and is—working in the name of His Son and through His Holy Spirit to save the world from sin. Salvation is part of His plan. He loves His creation and is working to make the human race completely whole again. He is working to bring peace to everyone who trusts in Jesus who said "...my Father is working to this very day" and "this very day" was the Sabbath when Jesus uttered those words.

God was working on that Sabbath, in the person of Jesus, healing the sick. They should have queried Him about how a man from Podunk could do such an amazing miracle, not about the timing of it. It was hard for them to accept the fact that there was a flaw in their system of theology.

---

[12] Mark 2:23
[13] Vine's Expository Dictionary of the New Testament
[14] Matthew 12:11-12

III

Do you see why Jesus came from Heaven and was willing to leave a place of sheer Paradise? God's chosen people, the Jews, had it all wrong. The leadership was hung up on the word "work" which they defined as "activity" and as a result were imposing heavy burdens on the people.[15] Jesus was reminding them that doing good on the Sabbath was not to be defined as work but as acts of love. Such acts are good because they are other-directed-activities. The Jews believed non-work that is self-directed earned them merits with God. God however takes note of "acts of love" that Paul defines as the heart of the Gospel.[16] Jesus came to show us that His Heavenly Father's view is quite different than that of those who insist on a worldview that lists works as a means of gaining favor with God.

Now back to Jesus' comment. As to the first two words, "My Father," please, understand that the Jews really did get the point. When they heard Him claiming Yahweh (Jehovah) as His Father, no doubt they put their fingers in their ears and began yelling in protest because they believed they were hearing blasphemy.

> "For this reason therefore the Jews were seeking all the more
> to kill Him, because He not only was breaking the Sabbath,
> but also was calling God His own Father, making Himself
> equal with God."[17]

Look again at those last five words; they got His message for sure! They complained to Pilate saying those were Jesus' very words. They saw this as sufficient basis for His execution. They complained to Pilate: "We have a law, and by that law He ought to die because He made Himself out to be the Son of God."[18] The Pharisees got something right but it made them angry because this would not fit into their closed system of theology! When they apprehended Jesus and first took him to the Sanhedrin, the official ruling body allowed by the Romans, they charged Jesus with heresy; they heard clearly what Jesus was saying as Luke records two charges:

---

[15] Matthew 23:4, Luke 11:46
[16] 1 Corinthians 13
[17] John 5:18
[18] John 19:7

"If You are the Christ, tell us." But He said to them, "If I tell you, you will not believe; and if I ask a question, you will not answer. But from now on the Son of Man will be seated at the right hand of the power of God." And they all said, "Are You the Son of God, then?" And He said to them, "Yes, I am."[19] Mark records that the high priest tore his clothes at this point[20] while the crowd shouted, "What further need do we have of testimony? For we have heard it ourselves from His own mouth."[21]

Then they bound Jesus and took Him to Pilate. Pilate was not interested in Jewish disputes, so the argument of blasphemy was immaterial to him. But when they accused Jesus of treason, that was another matter altogether. They were saying, "We found this man misleading our nation and forbidding to pay taxes to Caesar, and saying that He Himself is Christ, a King."[22] Pilate did not find Jesus guilty of treason, but according to John's Gospel, the people standing outside the judgment hall were shouting, "We have a law, and by that law He ought to die because He made Himself out to be the Son of God."[23] Yes, they certainly understood what Jesus was teaching and they vehemently disapproved. To say that this was a Man whose Father was God was beyond both their reason and their imagination.

Martha understood who Jesus was. Here's the exchange between Jesus and Martha after the death of her brother Lazarus:

Jesus said to her, "I am the resurrection and the life. He who believers in me will live again, even though he dies; and whoever lives and believes in me will never die. Do you believe this?" "Yes, Lord," she told him, "I believe that you are the Christ, the Son of God, who was to come into the world."[24]

John concludes the first twenty chapters (there are twenty-one altogether) explaining that he selected events in the life of Jesus to prove one thing, that Jesus was God's Son, the Man from Heaven, who came to become our Savior:

---

[19] Luke 22:67-70
[20] Mark 14:63
[21] Luke 22:71, see also Matthew 16:63-65
[22] Luke 23:2
[23] John 19:7
[24] John 11:25-27

> Therefore many other signs Jesus also performed in the presence of the disciples, which are not written in this book; but these have been written so that you may believe that Jesus is the Christ, the Son of God; and that believing you may have life in His name. [25]

The leaders saw Jesus as too much of a threat. They were suspicious despite the volume of Old Testament history and prophecies that talked about the Messiah to come. Perception of their coming Messiah precluded any man from Podunk who described Himself as "gentle and humble in heart!"[26] They could not see Jesus as the fulfillment of those prophecies. Sadly, they covered those Scriptures over with such a thick layer of regulations that they could no longer see their plain meaning. Since there were false prophets in Jesus' day, the Jewish leaders had to be cautious. And, no, they were not about to be had!

Sadder still, they held on to the Podunk theory until the day Jesus died! No one bothered to check that one small detail that Joseph and Mary were both of the line of David and Jesus was indeed born in Bethlehem. Thanks to Quirinius, the governor at the time of Jesus' birth, Jesus was also born in Bethlehem![27] Details, details! But how important they were! And still are!

Jesus was literate and so were many of the Jewish men of Jesus' day. On one occasion in the Nazareth synagogue, Jesus read from the scroll of the prophet Isaiah. He then sat down and said that the Scriptures He had just read were fulfilled that very day. It was obvious He was applying that prophecy to Himself. The men in the synagogue understood what Jesus was implying and reacted immediately with anger. They pushed Him out of the synagogue and began to run Him out of town. What He said was blasphemy! They were so angry they forced him to the cliff at the edge of town that they might push Him over the edge. He escaped out of their hands.[28]

Following this incident and because of the hardness of the hearts of people of Nazareth, He left there and dwelled in Capernaum[29] about thirty miles away ("as the crow flies").

At one point before His death, He said to the Jews, "I and the Father are One" and they picked up stones to stone Him. He said to them, "I showed

---

[25] John 20:20-31
[26] Matthew 11:29
[27] Luke 2
[28] Luke 4:29-30
[29] Matthew 4:13

you many good works from the Father; for which of them are you stoning Me?" The Jews answered Him, "For a good work we do not stone You, but for blasphemy; and because You, being a man, make Yourself out to be God."[30] Yes, they got it!

IV

Unlike the visitor to Ouarkoye who promised good news and delivered bad news, Jesus proved to be the best news ever since He was God incarnate in the flesh. John, the disciple "whom Jesus loved," conveys that very message as he begins his Gospel. [31] Here is his statement about the deity of Jesus: "In the beginning was the Word and the Word was with God, and the Word was God. He was in the beginning with God." "With God…was God," John wrote. [32] He got the message and so did all the other disciples who went everywhere proclaiming this amazing truth. They were willing even to die for it!

Greek scholars agree the phrase should read, "and the Word was God" and not as cults would have it, "the word was a god."

A few verses later, John says it clearly: "He was in the world, and the world was made through Him, and the world did not know Him." Further on in his first chapter, John makes the issue crystal clear when he says, "The Word became flesh, and dwelt among us, and we saw His glory, glory as of the only begotten from the Father, full of grace and truth."[33] John is talking about Jesus.

John quotes Jesus as saying this about Himself, "For I have come down from heaven, not to do My own will, but the will of Him who sent Me."[34] Later, in this same message, Jesus explains that the Jews' ancestors received manna in the wilderness but that bread did not assure them of eternal life. He now presents Himself to them as the living bread. "I am the living bread that came down out of heaven; if anyone eats of this bread, he will live forever; and the bread also which I will give for the life of the world is My flesh."[35] How

---

[30] John 10:33-34
[31] John 13:23; 20:2; 21:7, 20
[32] John 1:1-2
[33] John 1:14
[34] John 6:38
[35] John 6:51

could this good Man from Podunk say that and promise eternal life unless He, like the manna, "came down out of heaven."

The writer of the book of Hebrews lays out a résumé of the Man-from-Heaven for Jewish believers who are new to the faith—and for believers everywhere. The writer sets forth the theme, "Christ is better than…" and then fills in the rest of that statement with words like, "better than the prophets," "better than the angels," "better than Moses," and so on. Why is this Man, Jesus, better than all heavenly hosts and all the earthly saints? Why is He so amazing? Because He is the man from heaven.

Here are four statements that tell us quite convincingly that Jesus was more than the Man from Podunk, even if He did grow up there. A fifth quote from John makes it crystal clear what important truth Jesus was revealing to them. They got it! These marvelous statements from the book of Hebrews and the Gospel of John paint a magnificent picture of the man from heaven aka, Son of God.

1. Hebrews 1:2 says, "By (Jesus), (God) made the worlds." Jesus (along with the Father and the Spirit) created the world.

   Paul wrote to the Colossians (1:16), "For by him [Jesus] were all things created, that are in heaven, and that are in earth, visible and invisible, whether [they be] thrones, or dominions, or principalities, or powers: all things were created by him, and for him."

2. Hebrews 1:3 says. Jesus is "upholding all things by the word of his power." Jesus (along with the Father and the Spirit) is the sustainer of the world.

   The New Living Translation puts the phrase this way: He (Jesus) "sustains everything by the mighty power of his command."

Those who call themselves "deists" believe God created the world, but they do not believe God sustains it or involves Himself in the activities of the world. Some are extraordinarily brilliant, like Thomas Jefferson and do not believe this, but here it is in Scripture, and it couldn't be clearer! Jefferson resolved the issue to his satisfaction by cutting portions out of the Bible with which he did not agree. Notice how powerful the entire verse is:

[God] has spoken to us by His Son, whom He appointed heir of all things, through whom also He made the world who, being the brightness of [his] glory, and the express image of his person, and upholding all things by the word of his power, when he had by himself purged our sins, sat down on the right hand of the Majesty on high.

3. Hebrews 1:3 also says, He "purged our sins."[36] Jesus is the Redeemer of the world. This was the purpose of His coming. If He had been simply the Man from Podunk, this would have been entirely out of His realm. He had to be the Man from Heaven to deliver His creation from the clutches of Satan. He Himself had to be free from sin if He was going to lay His life down for the sins of mankind. He had to be willing to be the substitute. He also had to be fully man to identify with the human race. For that reason, He laid aside His prerogatives of deity[37] until His resurrection from the dead. His exceptional behavior while on earth was not the result of hanging on to His divine nature, but His total dependence on the Holy Spirit.

    Sin requires death; the forgiveness of sin requires a sacrifice. Jesus the Messiah therefore became the substitutionary sacrifice and died in our place. When we accept this truth and receive Jesus as our Savior, God welcomes us into His family because the sin that was a wall between God and us has been torn down. For the Jews, the image is not one of a wall, but one of the drape or curtain (called "a veil" in the King James Version) that was hanging in the temple between the Holy of Holies and the Holy Place. It was torn from top to bottom when Jesus died and the Holy of Holies, the place of the presence of God, was now open to all who receive the sacrifice of Jesus as a substitution for the death they would suffer had He not died. The culture of the New Testament knew about slaves sold in the market. That metaphor is also used of sinners who are slaves to sin. Jesus blood, that is, His death, is the ransom price paid so that believers may be redeemed and set free!

4. Hebrews 1:8 says, "But about the Son [God] says, 'Your throne, O God, will last forever and ever, and righteousness will be the scepter of your kingdom." Obviously, a kingdom of righteousness is founded on righteousness, and is characterized by righteousness, flourishing

---

[36] Hebrews 1:3
[37] See Philippians 2:5-8

forever! The heavenly program God has designed for our salvation will culminate with the crowning of our Lord and Savior, the Man from Podunk aka the Man from Heaven, as King of kings and Lord of lords.

What can we take from this? First, Jesus is deity. Does that mean that we have two gods, or perhaps three if one considers the Holy Spirit? No, the Jews have it right; we have one God. The Old Testament is very clear about that. We have a God who expresses Self in three Persons: Father, Son, and Holy Spirit. Each of the three Persons is identical with the other two in nature. For example, each one is eternal, holy, omnipresent, and omniscient. In this, they are One. In God's plan to save us from our sins, the One God played three roles: the Father who requires death to atone for sin; the Son who agreed to play the tragic, painful role as the perfect sacrifice; and the Spirit to guide believers into all truth.

Second, God's plan was that the Father, Son, and Holy Spirit, would be totally victorious over Satan, who temporarily succeeded in derailing creation for his wicked purposes. The Apostle Peter tells us God is not willing that anyone should perish. He wrote this: "The Lord is not slow in keeping his promise, as some understand slowness. He is patient with you, not wanting anyone to perish, but everyone to come to repentance."[38] Hence, Jesus, the Messiah, came to deliver not only the Jews but the Gentiles—and all the rest of us.

Look at it this way: God has a lifeboat on the rough seas of life. It's big enough to take in anyone who wants to be saved from the churning waters. Jesus urged His disciples to continue to scout the seas for every last person who desires to be saved. According to the book of Revelation, there will be some from every tribe and every nation. God will not force anyone into His lifeboat, but will plead with you to come near and He will help you reach a life preserver. That life preserver is the Man from Heaven; He will bring you to the boat. You don't need to keep struggling with life. This Man from Heaven has come into this world precisely to help those who are treading water. He will help you get in.

Having laid out the claims of Jesus the Messiah, and telling us the importance of the Son of God, the writer of the book of Hebrews goes on to say there is no comparison between Jesus and the angels: Jesus is better, far, far better. The writer quotes from Psalm 2, 102, 104, 110, as well as Moses

---

[38] New International Version

and Samuel, to prove his point. He clearly shows that Jesus Christ is not to be confused with angels—He was not and is not an angel; He is better than they.

God never calls the angels His sons but He calls Jesus His Son. God never commands us to worship angels, but He commands the angels to worship His Son—which, by the way, is another proof of the deity of the Son.[39] Deity is to be worshiped but when anything else is worshiped, that is idolatry.

Having discussed Jesus, the Son of Mary, and Jesus, the Son of God, there is something that needs to be made crystal clear. Jesus was of the nature of God before He was Mary's Son, and was of the nature of God after He arose from the dead. However, scripture is clear that while on earth, walking among the Jews, he thought and acted as a human being, not as God. Proof of this statement is found in Philippians 2. The NIV translation says it well:

> In your relationships with one another, have the same mindset as Christ Jesus: Who, being in very nature God, did not consider equality with God something to be used to his own advantage; rather, he made himself nothing by taking the very nature of a servant, being made in human likeness. And being found in appearance as a man, he humbled himself by becoming obedient to death— even death on a cross![40]

Yes, He was always God, but He chose to live as a one hundred percent human being and was able to be in the right place at the right time, do miracles, and speak the very words of God because He was filled with the Holy Spirit, was guided by the Spirit, and demonstrated the fruit of the Spirit in His life. He is our godly role model, this Man from Nazareth (Podunk), this Man from Heaven (His Father's House).

---

[39] Hebrews 1:5-6
[40] Philippians 2:5-8

[Be] like-minded, having the same love,
being one in spirit and of one mind.
Do nothing out of selfish ambition
or vain conceit.
Rather, in humility value others
above yourselves,
not looking to your own interests
but each of you
to the interests of the others.
In your relationships with one another,
have the same mindset as Christ Jesus...[95]

---

[41] Philippians 2:2-5

CHAPTER 3

SALVATION! PERFECT TIMING!

"The Fullness of Time"

I

Why was Jesus born two millennia ago? Why not 1000 AD or 2000 AD? Why not last December?

With the development of telecommunications in the twentieth and twenty-first centuries, wouldn't now have been a better time? To the merchant and the investor, time is money. To Americans, timing is everything. With all the hoopla and fear ushering in the year 2000, that would have been a great time for Jesus' birth, wouldn't it? How dramatic that would have been! In the midst of the heightened expectation would have come the bold headline on January 1, 2000: **JESUS CHRIST — BORN TODAY!**

Really? With all our emphasis on time, our minds are so cluttered, so filled with the constant flow of new electronic gadgets and the flood of knowledge from the Internet, we often need to pause a moment to ask ourselves which day of the week it is! If we write a letter, we search for a calendar to verify the date. The irony is that most Americans wear a watch and many have several timepieces, appointment books, and calendars throughout their homes.

If Jesus were an itinerant evangelist today, He would confront us as He did the Pharisees and Sadducees who demanded He give them a miraculous sign. There are those of us who would demand the same thing! He would say to us what He said to them, "You know the saying, 'Red sky at night means fair weather tomorrow; red sky in the morning means foul weather all day.' You know how to interpret the weather signs in the sky, but you don't know how to interpret the signs of the times!"[1] We have had the Bible in the English language since 1611 A.D. Do we know how to interpret the signs of the times?

When it comes to time, the American culture is quite different than third world countries where timepieces are rarer. I once asked a schoolboy in Burkina Faso, West Africa, "What time is it?" He had some instruction about time but never owned a watch. He stretched his arm up towards heaven and gave me an approximate time. He was correct as to the hour but had no way of telling the minutes. Why should he? His culture wasn't in a hurry, nor was "time money" to his tribal fathers. As to time, sunrise and sunset—when it was time to get up and time to go to bed—mattered. As to seasons, when the rains start and when they quit—mattered. Minutes had no relevance.

We of Western culture can even boast about the creation of an atomic clock and its latest improvements. CNN Online published the following headline: "Major Boost in Atomic Clock Accuracy: Loses Or Gains Less Than A Second Every 300 Million Years." But a later report based on an NIST report claims: "The new strontium clock is so precise it would neither gain nor lose one second in about 5 billion years, if it could operate that long."[2]

Apparently, God is not as interested in minutes and seconds as we are. He didn't create diverse timepieces; man did. God doesn't need to wear a wristwatch. He created the sun, moon and stars and that was an *event* not according to a timepiece with a pendulum swinging somewhere in space; I repeat, it was an *event*.

This observation leads to a major point: *events are more important to God than time*. This point is important to remember as you read the Scriptures, especially the twenty-fourth chapter of Matthew. When His disciples asked Him about the time of "the end," presumably the time of His enthronement as King, His response was to give a series of events, not a time frame even though they asked the question "When?".

God's reference is not the atomic clock but Himself. His agenda was—and still is—to rescue the human race from Satan's domination. Satan gained

---

[1] Matthew 16:1-3 NLT
[2] National Institute of Standards and Technology (NIST)

control of human hearts in the Garden of Eden. The Bible reveals that God's agenda consists of multiple-times and multiple-events. Additionally, every event during the Old Testament epoch, in some way, points back to God and forward to the perfection of His plan that was agreed upon in the divine council before time began.[3] Every revealed truth has something to do with Jesus Christ's life, the pivotal point in history.

God is alive and well in all time zones simultaneously; He doesn't need to refer to Greenwich Mean Time. Nor is He ever troubled by jet lag. God created the solar system and knows exactly how He planned it to function and how long it will function. He's kept track of it for thousands of years and has never missed an appointment! His clock and His calendar are perfect. They coincide with His planned events.

All the little events, as well as the big stories found in the Old Testament, led up to God's great event, the giving up of His Son, Jesus, to die on the cross. God determined He should become the ultimate sacrifice on behalf of mankind. God didn't have to bother with sin or sinners, but His love caused Him to create human beings and since Eden, to save human beings at any cost. And what a cost! Jesus died on the cross a horrible death—to pay the penalty for sins of others—He was never guilty of sin—and His sacrifice of Himself affects every living soul.[4] All the sacrifices under the Law of Moses were symbolic of the great sacrifice to come, that of Jesus on the cross.

How does God view time since He lives outside of time and is never bound by it? One clue might be television broadcasts that are not bound by time zones so that major world events like the Olympics can be seen live worldwide. Such broadcasts are often labeled as "real time" rather than "recorded time" or "virtual time." Hurrah for satellites well placed in the sky!

What will God use to herald the second coming of His Son Jesus since every eye will see His return? In the Old Testament, God used the weather on numerous occasions to punish sinners. He created it; He can use it! He also increased the silent forces that exist in our atmosphere and no doubt, He will use them! The promise is that "every eye will see" the Son of God, the Man of Eternity, at His reentry into our time and space. That is contrary to some

---

[3] John 17:24, 1 Peter 1:20
[4] Romans 3:23, "for all have sinned and fall short of the glory of God,"

of the cults that say He has already come and is biding His time *somewhere* before presenting Himself. The Scripture is clear:

> "Look, he is coming with the clouds," and "every eye will see him, even those who pierced him"; and all peoples on earth "will mourn because of him." So shall it be! Amen.[5]

Those quotes within the quote above are from the Old Testament books of Daniel and Zechariah, respectively.

Broadcast bands are not restricted by time zones and can penetrate all zones at the same time (with only a slight lag). If radio waves can do that, are we to suppose a sovereign God is less knowledgeable or less powerful? By no means! Jesus' second advent will be proof God is all of that and more. "Every eye" will see Him and many will mourn and weep because they, like the six foolish virgins,[6] will not be ready to meet the King on the greatest day of joy and celebration the world has ever known—joy without end, not the temporary happiness when one's team wins the super bowl or one's daughter has been crowned Miss Universe.

II

God did not take our calendar and assign December 25 and say in the Council in Heaven, "Let's see if this particular day works."

So what time was it according to God's plan when He said Mary would bear the Christ Child? We have no clue in the Gospels or Epistles as to the date and time of Jesus' birth—we need to accept the fact that time was irrelevant. Astronomers, archaeologists, and theologians have tried to fill in the gap but have been unsuccessful.

What was important enough to call the wise men from the East and poor shepherds from the fields? It was an event that both groups witnessed, each seeing a different display in the heavens. We know that He was to be born in Bethlehem despite the fact that his mother was a resident of Nazareth. And we know the more important fact that the event did occur and shepherds and the chorus of angels, and the Magi and a star have testified to it. Yes, it was the glorious event that was relevant, an event destined to alter history.

---

[5] Revelation 1:7, the first quote is from Daniel 7:13 and the second from Zechariah 12:10
[6] Matthew 25:11-13

The Church Fathers in the latter part of the fourth century decided the church needed a day to celebrate Jesus' birth, and the day designated by them was December 25. That day became the feast day for the celebration of the Festival of the Nativity, or Christmas.

If the exact date doesn't matter—and it doesn't—why did God ordain that the event should happen when it did? Checking the Scriptures, there is a reference to God's timing found in the Epistle to the Galatians. Here are the words, "in the fullness of time." That may not satisfy the American mind, but is an important phrase in the Bible and should not to go unnoticed.

> But when the fullness of the time came, God sent forth His Son, born of a woman, born under the Law, so that He might redeem those who were under the Law, that we might receive the adoption as sons.[7]

This was not a chance event. Centuries unfolded contributing to the planning of this major world event. The importance of the word *fullness* is this: it tells us nothing lacked when God broke into time for Christ's birth. Every last detail proclaimed by the prophets had to fall into place and every detail did! Careful study of the Old Testament indicates that's exactly what happened.

Take note that this is precisely what will happen at another world event, Christ's second coming. When every piece of prophecy relating to His second coming is finally in place, Jesus Christ will break through the clouds and make His appearance as King of kings and Lord of lords!

If that is true—and it is—shouldn't we be able to figure out the *time* of His coming? The answer is no. Despite all the prophecies concerning His first coming, no Jewish scholar could figure out the exact time of His arrival. He took them by surprise. And that is exactly what will happen at His second coming! Jesus said that is a fact. His coming, He said, will be like a thief in the night![8]

Remember, the key word is event *not* time. For His second coming, gather the Scriptures about the events that are leading up to the coming grand event, and most importantly, be ready!

Wouldn't it have been simpler for God to annihilate Satan after Satan caused Adam and Eve to fall into sin? The answer is no. God created Adam and Eve that His love might find fulfillment and that required those that He created to have a free will; He did not make them robots.

---

[7] Galatians 4:4
[8] Luke 12:35-40

Destroying Satan at that time would not have redeemed our first parents nor any of us who followed them over the centuries. Because of their act of disobedience in the Garden of Eden, every generation that followed was born with the option to do good or to do evil—and every generation has shown a preference to do the latter and not the former. In fact, men and women don't just prefer to sin; they soon become enslaved to it with no way out to freedom! Only Jesus is the answer.

III

Jesus' birth, life and ministry, as well as His death and resurrection, along with the coming of the Holy Spirit on the Day of Pentecost, all occurred "in the fullness of time." It is great to observe Palm Sunday, Good Friday, Easter Sunday, and Pentecost on their designated days, but it is the event not the day that is important.

Isaiah prophesied that the branch from the root of Jesse, King David's father, would bud and sprout green.[9] Isaiah never said precisely when Jesus, this descendent of David, would appear. The Apostle Paul, acknowledging God's sovereignty, affirms that Jesus was born "at the right time." He wrote, "For while we were still helpless, at the right time Christ died for the ungodly." [10]

The Old Testament is full of signs and symbols of the great event God had planned. That great event is the day God became flesh, also called "the Incarnation". His life and teaching were the fulfillment of every prophecy of every man and woman sent from God to encourage and also to warn his chosen people.

Suddenly, the prophecies of His first coming were fulfilled, culminating on Resurrection Day (Easter). It was then that He completed all that was prophesied concerning His first advent. This advent covered all that was necessary to make salvation available to everyone who believes God's word, which says that both Jews and Gentiles are sinners and deserve His judgment. However, there is salvation for all in the name of Jesus. God, in His compassion, provided an escape route for all sinners from an eternity in the Lake of Fire. Creating that escape route is what His Son Jesus came to do.

Anyone who has a problem believing the events of the New Testament needs to pay close attention to what was prophesied from *c.* 2000 to *c.* 400

---

[9] Isaiah 11.1
[10] Romans 5:6

B.C. It's all there! It's laid out in a series of events that culminate gloriously in the manger at Bethlehem. For Christian believers, Bethlehem, Nazareth, and Jerusalem are all very important places because that is where the events about His first advent were fulfilled.

In a short time, the good news of these events spread throughout the known world even though it unfolded in just a limited geographical area: Nazareth to Jerusalem, eighty miles as the crow flies, and Bethlehem to Jerusalem, about five miles. Now the name of Jesus is known in every corner of the world!

Paul takes the many pieces of the prophetic puzzle and fits them beautifully into a cohesive whole in the Galatians passage quoted in Section II of this chapter. God's plan was recognized for what it is, a marvelous, fantastic love letter from God to the human race. Paul manages to put it altogether in a single sentence. It is from Galatians 4 and was quoted in the first section of this chapter. It bears repeating:

> But when the fullness of the time came, God sent forth His Son, born of a woman, born under the Law so that He might redeem those who were under the Law, that we might receive the adoption as sons.[11]

Pause, reflect, and see that God is a perfect planner! He saw to it that every detail was in place for this momentous event in human history. Amazing!

Don't fail to miss the end of Paul's sentence: "that we might receive the adoption as sons." That same God, our Heavenly Father, had a perfect plan and its purpose included every believer, including both Jew and Gentile. Imagine! God was planning to adopt us as sons and daughters and make us part of His family. If you are a believer, you have an elder brother and His name is Jesus. That, too, is amazing!

When their Messiah came, the Jews viewed Him as too meek and mild and one who broke the Sabbath laws. It was not "the fullness of time" as far as they were concerned. He was from the wrong town and He was a threat, so they connived and conspired to have Him crucified. They succeeded in their plans not knowing they were actually fulfilling Isaiah's prophecies about His suffering and death.[12]

---

[11] Galatians 4:4-5
[12] Isaiah 53

Writing to the Roman church, Paul explains the inclusion of the Gentiles and the temporary exclusion of the Jews who rejected Jesus as their Messiah. He uses the imagery of an olive tree:

> If some of the branches were broken off, and you [Gentiles], being a wild olive, were grafted in among them and became partaker with them of the rich root of the olive tree, do not be arrogant toward the branches; but if you are arrogant, remember that it is not you who supports the root, but the root supports you. You will say then, "Branches were broken off so that I might be grafted in." Quite right, they were broken off for their unbelief, but you stand by your faith. Do not be conceited, but fear…[13]

Persecution began in Jesus' day because the Jews had not done their homework well. Their erroneous hope of a political Messiah to deliver them from the heavy hand of Rome would disappoint and puzzle them.

IV

In summary, it was truly "the fullness of time" when a selfish, wicked and cruel Caesar Augustus unwittingly and unknowingly followed God's plan perfectly. Yes, even a pagan emperor was unable to thwart the will of God. Rather, he did exactly what God was planning at a time when the world would be the most prepared for Jesus Christ, the Savior of the world.

During the heyday of the Roman Empire, the spread of the Gospel message of salvation to the known world occurred quickly after the death and resurrection of Christ. Rome played into God's hands by the creation of *Pax Romana* that created a relatively safe empire for travelers.[14] And the wicked two-bit king Herod—that is how the emperor saw him—also played right into the hands of the great, righteous God of Heaven!

---

[13] Romans 11:17-20

[14] The term "Pax Romana" (Roman peace), refers to the time period from 27 BC to 180 AD in the Roman Empire. This 200-year period saw unprecedented peace and economic prosperity throughout the Empire, which spanned from England in the north to Morocco in the south and Iraq in the east. During this time, the Roman Empire reached its peak in land mass and population swelled (estimated 70 million). Retrieved from: http://www. USHistory.org/ancient civilizations

The completion of the Great Commission is one of the most important details of God's plan yet remaining. God's desire is to have the human race reconciled to Him, both Jew and Gentile and, when every tribe and nation has heard the Gospel, He will usher in Jesus' Second Advent.

This is the culmination of the events in Matthew twenty-four when Jesus responded to His disciples after they asked Him about the end. According to Luke's Gospel, they were not looking for an event; they were asking for a sign and a date: "When, Lord?" He responded that it would be related to a series of events, concluding with this grand event:

> This gospel of the kingdom shall be preached in the whole world as a testimony to all the nations, and then the end will come.[15]

The Jews prayed a long time for the Messiah to come. Christians, too, have been praying a long time for Jesus to come back. But God is waiting for that last piece of the puzzle to be dropped in: and that piece is apparently related to the proclamation of the gospel to every tribe and every nation. That last piece of the puzzle may well occur in a Podunk somewhere, at the location of some obscure tribe.

Jesus urged His disciples to be ready because the world will never know when the last tribe has been entered to hear the Gospel for the first time. His second coming is not like a salesman who calls and makes an appointment but rather like, according to His word, a "thief in the night."[16] A thief is one who comes silently and certainly unexpectedly!

Why is God waiting for the last tribe to hear? He has already given us the answer in the book of Revelation:

> After these things I looked, and behold, a great multitude which no one could count, from every nation and all tribes and peoples and tongues, standing before the throne and before the Lamb, clothed in white robes, and palm branches were in their hands; and they cry out with a loud voice, saying, "Salvation to our God who sits on the throne, and to the Lamb."[17]

---

[15] Matthew 24:14
[16] 1 Thessalonians 5:2; 2 Peter 3:10
[17] Revelation 7:10

Since we don't have God's clock or His calendar hanging on our wall, we must search the Scriptures; the clues are there. But don't be misled: we must look for events and not time.

When, then, will this Man, born in Bethlehem, raised in Nazareth (*aka* Podunk), and back residing in His Father's House in Heaven (while at the same time with us) come again? But wait! That's the wrong question! Ask this question: What final *event* will precede His Second Coming? That's the right question! The Lord told the disciples in His final word to them that it will be the completion of what we now call The Great Commission.

Dr. A. B. Simpson, founder of The Christian and Missionary Alliance, understood the Lord's words to be a call to missionary activity, and as a result, a glorious missionary movement came into existence! When that work is completed—every Christian's obligation, the fullness of time will be realized and He will break through the skies!

You may hear theologians say it is impossible for Jesus to come soon because linguists say there are many tribes who have not yet heard and that would take a long time to see that every tribe was reached. More than half a century ago, linguists told us there were "2000 tongues to go." It was the title of a book telling the early story of Wycliffe linguist/missionary organization.

They had the number wrong. Later surveys have shown the number to be at least 6000. However, those reached by early missionaries are now sending out missionaries on their own and in some lands, second-generation Christians are busy producing multiple radio programs in many languages.

Today, multiplication rather than addition is at work even in third world countries. The final event, the proclamation of the truth in Christ, is in high gear. As to the timing, that is safely locked up in the heart of the Father. Jesus' word to His disciples was this:

> "It is not for you to know times or epochs which the Father
> has fixed by His own authority."[18]

When He comes, let Him find us *doing*. If He should call us home before He returns, may He find us ready with our lamps still giving light.[19]

Jesus came *in the fullness of time* and He will come the second time *in the fullness of time*.

---

[18] Acts 1:7
[19] Matthew 25:4

CHAPTER 4

SAVED!

God's Comprehensive Plan

I

As a teenager, I was asked, "Are you saved?" I was surprised by the abruptness of the question and as a matter of fact, I had never heard anyone ask that question before. My answer was, "Yes." Of course, that is a good question but there was no follow-up question, "Are you being saved?" Nor was the question, "Do you have the assurance that you will be saved?"

Do these questions somehow seem inappropriate? Do you object and say, "Nobody ever asks questions like that! I got saved several years ago and I even know the date and place!"

Do the questions sound like heresy? To the contrary, these questions are backed by Scripture. There are past, present, and future aspects to salvation.

Christians tend to be content if a person responds to the first question, "Yes, I am saved. I went to the altar when I was 5 (or 14, or 52) and invited Christ into my life." With this affirmative reply, a follow-up question should be asked, "Are you now being saved?" The conversation should continue like this: "Praise the Lord that you are born again! You have been saved from the dominating power of sin that is the nature that the Apostle Paul calls the "old man" or "the old self."[1] This encounter with God is explained in detail in the next chapter. But there is more to explain here.

---

[1] Romans 6:6, Ephesians 4:22, Colossians 3:9

If one claims to be saved, that person's past includes a born again experience; technically, it is called regeneration. That's the past tense of salvation for that person and the subject of Chapter 5.

The present tense of salvation deals with a person's daily walk with the Lord. That's the subject of Chapter 6. This is the neglected aspect of salvation. An observation of another person's walk and listening to his or her talk will provide an answer as to whether there is spiritual growth. Walking according to the voice of the Spirit living within is called sanctification (also called holiness). The New Testament speaks often of this present aspect of salvation and we will explore its meaning and application in Chapter 6.

A parent doesn't have to ask a teenage son how he is growing. All the parent has to do is to check the length of his pants. Or take him to the shoe store and hear the clerk say, "He needs a size larger." My mother was never prepared for that comment or for the larger box the clerk brought out. She would exclaim upon seeing the larger box and the larger shoes, "Gunboats!" (I never got the connection, but I got the new shoes.)

As to spiritual growth, over time one can observe the behavior of another individual who claims to be a believer to see if there is development, "fruit," as Jesus called it.

We are told to "put on Christ", which refers to spiritual clothes.[2] Look for spiritual clothes; they are observable. Spiritual clothes are the fruit of the Spirit: "love, joy, peace, patience, kindness, goodness, faithfulness, gentleness, self-control."[3] The exercise of these values is observable behaviors.

To ask a newcomer at one's Christian youth group, "Are you saved?" can be misleading. The question should be "Have you been regenerated?" But since that sounds too theological, try this, "Have you been born again?" That is what the word "regenerated" means.

Regenerated and saved are not synonymous, however. That statement is extremely important to remember. Again, those two terms are not synonymous. Regeneration is part of the plan of salvation but it is not the whole of it. The term salvation is an umbrella term and the other term, regenerated, is more specifically, a subset of salvation. It is not wrong to use the one for the other, but it can be misleading. In Chapter 1 of his book, "Salvation," Louis Sperry

---

[2] Romans 13:14 and Ephesians 4:24
[3] Galatians 5:22-23

Chafer wrote the following; I have added in brackets the words he is referring to for clarification:[4]

> As used in the New Testament, the word salvation may indicate all [regeneration, sanctification, and glorification] or a part of the divine undertaking. When the reference is to all of the work of God, the whole transformation is in view from the estate wherein one is lost and condemned to the final appearance of that one in the image of Christ in glory. This larger use of the word [salvation], therefore, combines in it many separate works of God for the individual, such as Atonement, Grace, Propitiation, Forgiveness, Justification, Imputation, Regeneration, Adoption, Sanctification, Redemption and Glorification.

Chafer adds several words to his list that are all part of salvation, but salvation has three closely connected aspects or stages that are found under salvation's umbrella. They are *regeneration, sanctification,* and *glorification.* All three are available to the entire human race because of atonement, grace, propitiation, forgiveness, justification, imputation, adoption, and redemption. These words are associated with three major concepts found under salvation's umbrella. They are biblical concepts that are part of God's agenda for the human race, thanks to His Son, the Savior Jesus Christ. Why wouldn't Christians want to know all that God has provided and the terms the Bible uses to describe them?

Some contemporary writers are calling on Christians to forget these terms and speak more simply. This simple approach is acceptable in evangelism, but not if one is attempting to establish new believers. These terms provide handles for certain concepts of scriptural truth. No secular culture has a right to delete them because they never heard the terms before. And it is not okay for pastor-teachers to delete them because his or her congregation has never heard the terms. Believers should become familiar with them, rejoice over the marvelous plan of God they describe, and be thankful for all that had to be part of God's plan to allow us to have part in it! Such knowledge is a basis for "rational worship."[5]

Did you know that singing hymns is one way to learn more about these terms? Many hymns were written in an age when hymnbooks were scarce

---

[4] Salvation, Louis Sperry Chafer, Kregel Publications, a division of Kregel, Inc., Grand Rapids, MI, 1991
[5] Romans 12:1

items and being taught hymns was a marvelous way to teach theology. Of course, expository preaching is the most important method a teacher can use to explain these biblical concepts.

Because Christians don't recognize these terms is never a reason to throw them overboard. To learn them is to understand more about God and His great love for us.

Rev. Oswald J. Smith had it right in his hymn, "Saved!" Repeating the word "Saved!" three times, he covered the plan of salvation well.

> Saved! Saved! Saved! my sins are all forgiv'n;
>
> Christ is mine! I'm on my way to heav'n;
>
> Once a guilty sinner, lost, undone,
>
> Now a child of God, saved thro' His Son.[6]

Being "saved" is not a once-and-for-all event. Like life, salvation starts with birth and then is an ongoing series of spiritual events (growth). That is true for every faithful believer who is authenticating his or her faith. Christians need to keep in mind that "I'm saved!" starts, continues, and culminates in a grand finale! We are "Saved! [and] Saved! [and] Saved!" It is not "Saved!" (regenerated) three times. Rather it is Saved! from sin (regeneration); Saved! from self (sanctification); and Saved from the wrath of God to come (glorification).

Let me put it this way. The initial event is regeneration (i.e., I am saved!); the continuing events are sanctification (i.e., I am being saved!); and the crowning event will be glorification (i.e., I will be saved!).

"Once saved, always saved" is not a statement found in the Bible, nor is it an accurate statement when "saved" is used synonymously for *regeneration*. Regeneration is, as we have just noted, birth into a new life. "Once regenerated, always regenerated" is like saying, "once born, always born". That statement simply doesn't make sense. That phrase also doesn't refer to the whole plan of salvation since sanctification is in progress and glorification has not yet occurred.

Am I taking away a Christian's feeling of security? In one sense, yes, if one's security is based only on this phrase. No, if one has faith in the keeping power of a heavenly Father and the many promises in the Scriptures that tell us of His keeping power. Christians need to rely on God's promises in the

---

[6] "Saved!" Smith, O. J. (1917). Retrieved from http://cyberhymnal.org/htm/s/a/v/ saved.htm

Word *and to walk as Jesus walked.* Therein lies the security of the believer. The Christian is "secure in Christ," as a Bible college professor used to tell his students.

It's important to know that something very important follows *salvation-regeneration* something that Christians are to seek after on a daily basis. It is *salvation-sanctification.* How and when sanctification starts in the life of a believer is explained in a later chapter.

A cautionary note here: neither regeneration nor sanctification can be earned. The Apostle Paul wrote:

> For by grace you have been saved through faith; and that not
> of yourselves, it is the gift of God; not as a result of works,
> so that no one may boast.[7]

Salvation—the entire plan that includes regeneration, sanctification, and glorification—is a gift from God. When a gift is offered, the recipient has only to take it.

To evangelize is to proclaim the good news about Jesus Christ. That's the Great Commission Jesus entrusted to His disciples in Matthew twenty-eight. But that's only half of Christ's message. Have we forgotten the second part of the Great Commission found in Matthew 28:20? Jesus also said, "teaching them to observe all that I commanded you." That relates to growth and that's sanctification.

Many early missionaries saw themselves as evangelists and appropriately so. They were going to areas where people had never heard the name of Jesus. As a result of their faithfulness, many small churches were formed. Throughout their missionary careers, they kept evangelizing. What was needed was the next wave of pastor-teachers. There is still a great need for evangelists to go to the many tribes yet to hear that Jesus died for their sins. There are also many church groups, some small and some very large, that need the Bible to be translated into their languages and require teaching to keep them on the sanctification track.

Here in America, I have heard messages delivered to men being ordained to a public ministry as pastors. The charge to the about-to-be-ordained pastors was structured almost completely as if they were going to be evangelists. The newly ordained ministers went on to assume the title of pastor, and churches hired them as pastors—but expected them to function as evangelists.

---

[7] Ephesians 2:7-8

43

Congregations and pastors alike believe it is the role of the pastor to increase the numbers of attendees at the Sunday morning worship services and Sunday School classes. Confusing, isn't it!

There are to be evangelists ordained and sent forth by the church to share Christ with unbelievers. True, it is also the calling of every believer but there are particular individuals who, having the gift for evangelism, should be ordained as such and supported by the church. In the past, they were poorly supported by the church and the role of evangelist has been left to television personalities who can raise funds by using the medium and writing books.

The office of pastor is separate from the office of evangelist, according to the Word of the Lord. In the twentieth century, there were evangelists who were called to have revival meetings in local churches. Congregants were expected to invite unbelievers to the services. However, by using the word "revival," the intent was also to revive lethargic Christians. I don't think it is possible to call unbelievers to faith in Christ and teach believers about sanctification, all in the same one-hour service. Confusing, isn't it!

> He gave some *as* apostles, and some *as* prophets, and some *as* evangelists, and some *as* pastors-teachers for the equipping of the saints for the work of service, to the building up of the body of Christ.[8]

Illiterate Christians are untaught (unfed), but happily, the situation can be reversed before the flock—Christians—die of malnutrition! The purpose of this book is to provide "meat and potatoes" for hungry Christians, that is, to provide illiterate Christians with food that will result in understanding the Word. This is the key to joy that results in being effective witnesses for Christ. That means believers must understand basic terms like "salvation," "baptized with water," "baptized in the Holy Spirit," "filled with the Spirit" and other topics necessary if one's faith is to be authenticated and one's testimony is to be clear when shared. These concepts are explained in this book.

II

The Sunday evening evangelistic service in evangelical churches was the time devoted to calling unbelievers to faith in Christ. The intent was to "get them saved." While there, the Holy Spirit would often convict them of

---

[8] Ephesians 4:12

their sin and conviction impelled them to go to forward to the altar when the invitation was given at the conclusion of the message. They would pray to receive Christ as their Savior and Lord. That certainly was a *salvation* experience! "Praise the Lord, brother! You just got saved!"

Amen! Yes, you can call that salvation, but more precisely, that is a born again or a regeneration experience. It is not salvation in the full sense of the term. New believers should never be given the impression that this special and wonderful event got them squared away with the Lord and there is nothing further to be concerned about except regular attendance at the church's services, pray and read their Bibles.

Unfortunately, rather than exegete the Word—most do not have the training to do so—Sunday School teachers tell interesting Bible stories and exhort their classes to read their Bibles and become part of the church's ministries.

Sunday School teachers and pastors unfortunately convey the impression, albeit unintentionally, that going forward and calling it "getting saved" is the whole plan of salvation. Preaching evangelistic messages rather than accept the more difficult role of being pastor-teachers indicates to the newly converted that their job is to go and recruit others for the Lord. Those recruited are exhorted to go and recruit more recruiters.

Teaching new converts lessons on how to evangelize is seen as primary when they should be taught first how to live a holy (that is, sanctified) life. They should understand that they must move from salvation-regeneration into salvation-sanctification.

Just like converts on the mission field who need follow up, there must be follow up for American converts as well. They need pastor-teachers to instruct them that there is more truth to be learned if one is to "walk as Jesus walked." New believers—and many who have been in the church a long time—need to know how to apply the truth they are hearing. It is a dangerous thing for evangelists to leave new believers without proper instruction. Evangelists hope pastor-teachers will follow up, but it does not appear to be so since "Christians are illiterate," as George Barna discovered.

Regeneration must be followed by sanctification! That teaching should begin right away. The first cry of a newborn is delightful; parents rejoice in every sound their baby makes. Quickly, these sweet sounds turn to inconsolable cries as the baby demands to be fed. Parents comply with these demands and then rejoice over every added inch and pound gained by their new offspring! Growth is essential and, if there is to be growth, there must be regular feedings.

Like hungry babies, Christians need to be fed for growth. However, I fear that they don't recognize their own "hunger pains" which is why I rejected the idea of "meat and potatoes for Hungry Christians" as a potential title for this book. Moreover, I believe many Christians don't know they have hunger pains for the "meat and potatoes" of the Word. They think those pains are a cry for some new electronic gadget, a better job, a nicer house, or perhaps a more emotional experience.

Materialism wasn't a big factor in Peter's day except for a very few people. He makes reference, rather, to attitudes when he says:

> Therefore, putting aside all malice and all deceit and hypocrisy and envy and all slander, like newborn babies, long for (or, crave) the pure milk of the word, so that by it you may grow in respect to salvation.[9]

In that first one-time event, spiritual birth, one's spirit is made alive and this new spiritual life has direct access to God through Jesus Christ.[10] This new life produces spiritual sensibilities including taste: "O taste and see that the Lord is good."[11]

The first aspect infuses new life into our dead spirit according to Ephesians 2. The second aspect infuses life into the soul, that is, the heart and mind of the individual and deals with the Christian's value system.[12] The third step infuses new life into the physical body after death when the body is glorified according to 1 Corinthians 15.

This is God's plan: new life first for the spirit, second for the soul, and third, for the physical body. All this is possible through Jesus Christ and in His name alone. Hunger in unbelievers will intensify when they see the example of a growing Christian, obedient to the Lord and Christlike in behavior.

---

[9] 1 Peter 2:2

[10] Ephesians 2:18: Paul is saying both Jews (God's chosen people) and the Gentiles have access to the Father

[11] Psalm 34:8

[12] Romans 12:2: the purpose of the renewal of the mind is found in the same verse, so that you may prove what the will of God is, that which is good and acceptable and perfect.

III

To recap, let us remember salvation has three aspects or stages. In the New Testament, the Greek word, to save, is *sozo*. Paul uses three tenses of sozo to explain the past experience of a believer (I am saved!), the present experience of a believer (I am being saved!), and the future experience of a believer (I will be saved!). Here are some biblical texts from Paul's letters.

1. Past tense

    Romans 8:24, For in hope we **have been saved**, but hope that is seen is not hope; for who hopes for what he already sees?

    Ephesians 2:8, For by grace you **have been saved** through faith; and that not of yourselves, it is the gift of God.

2. Present tense

    1 Corinthians 1:18, For the word of the cross is foolishness to those who are perishing, but to us who **are being saved** it is the power of God.

    2 Corinthians 2:15, For we are a fragrance of Christ to God among those who **are being saved** and among those who are perishing.

    Philippians 2:12, So then, my beloved, just as you have always obeyed, not as in my presence only, but now much more in my absence, **work out your salvation** with fear and trembling.

3. Future tense

    Romans 5:9-10, Much more then, having now been justified by His blood, we **shall be saved** from the wrath of God through Him. For if while we were enemies we were reconciled to God through the death of His Son, much more, having been reconciled, we [believers] **shall be saved** by His life.

    Romans 10:9, that if you confess with your mouth Jesus as Lord, and believe in your heart that God raised Him from the dead, you **will be saved**.

There are four important facts to highlight about God's marvelous gift, providing Christians with solid reasons to rejoice. Here they are:

FIRST, sin has "wages" (death), but God's gift (eternal life) is a gift freely bestowed on those who believe that Jesus died for their sins. Human beings have no merits of their own, but receive the gift of salvation—in its fullest sense—because of the merits of Jesus Christ who paid the penalty (death) on their behalf. God accepts that substitution. Children of Adam, we are all sinners! Romans 3:23 and 6:23 spell out the transaction:

> For the wages of sin is death, but the free gift of God is eternal life in Christ Jesus our Lord[13]

> For by grace you have been saved through faith; and that not of yourselves, it is the gift of God. [14]

SECOND, at regeneration, we are declared to be both holy and righteous. Sanctification is the process whereby we become holy and righteous. When Luke talks about Zacharias and Elizabeth, he gives a definition of the word "righteous."

> They were both righteous in the sight of God, walking blamelessly in all the commandments and requirements of the Lord.

THIRD, according to John 3:16, every Christian possesses God's gift of eternal life right now. It is not something that is given to the Christian at death as though it were a ticket to get into heaven. I return to that beautiful verse, John 3:16, once again: the present tense is used in the passage in connection with the promise to those having believed. Meditate on the verbs "believe" and "have" (a present experience) and rejoice over the connection between them. If you are a believer, you possess eternal life right now!

> For God so loved the world that He gave His only begotten Son, that whoever believes in Him shall not perish, but have eternal life.

FOURTH, read the marvelous passage that Paul shared with the Corinthian church—and with us. (See gray box.) God has so much

---

[13] Romans 3:23
[14] Romans 6:23

more for believers who are willing to lay the milk aside, begin on solid food, and grow up!

> Yet when I am among mature believers, I do speak with words of wisdom, but not the kind of wisdom that belongs to this world or to the rulers of this world, who are soon forgotten. No, the wisdom we speak of is the mystery of God—his plan that was previously hidden, even though he made it for our ultimate glory before the world began. But the rulers of this world have not understood it; if they had, they would not have crucified our glorious Lord.
>
> That is what the Scriptures mean when they say:
> "No eye has seen, no ear has heard,
> and no mind has imagined
> what God has prepared for those who love him."
> But it was to us that God revealed these things by his Spirit.
> For his Spirit searches out everything and shows us God's deep secrets.
> No one can know a person's thoughts except that person's own spirit, and no one can know God's thoughts except God's own Spirit.

Every Christian, having received God's Spirit dwelling within, can know the wonderful things God has prepared for His children.

CHAPTER 5

SAVED FROM SIN!

Born Twice

I

In the previous chapter, we learned there are three aspects or stages to salvation: regeneration, sanctification, and glorification.

We also learned that believing salvation and regeneration (being born again) to be identical experiences is false and misleading. Occasionally in the Scriptures, the word salvation is used to describe regeneration; that is, the whole is used for the part. Yes, regeneration is also salvation, but to confuse them—as is often done—does serious damage to Christian growth. The last fifty years of church history and the illiteracy issue prove the point.

We start our study of salvation-regeneration with a summary statement:

> REGENERATION
> is the first aspect of salvation,
> meaning "born again" or
> "born from above";
> that's when life is given to our dead spirits.

This chapter will show that salvation-regeneration is distinct from the remaining two aspects (salvation-sanctification and salvation-glorification) and is foundational for the other two. Several questions will be answered in this chapter, questions that address Why? What? and How?

First, however, let me repeat: all three aspects or stages of salvation are God's doing and there is nothing anyone can do to earn, buy, or demand them as a reward for good behavior. The death of Jesus Christ has made it possible that all this could be a gift from a God who loves His fallen creation and gave His Son to redeem it.

> All are justified freely by his grace through the redemption
> that came by Christ Jesus.[1]

Now, on to answer some questions that inevitably arise when discussing this incredible work of God.

II

The first question is "Why do we need to be born again?" That's a very easy question to answer. In John 3, Jesus told Nicodemus that it was necessary: "You must be born again." Nicodemus came to Jesus at night seeking further information about who Jesus really was. In John 3:3, Jesus addresses the question of "why". His full statement to Nicodemus is this, "Truly, truly, I say to you, unless one is born again he cannot see the kingdom of God." Therefore, born again is key to seeing—and thereby knowing about—the kingdom of God.

Nicodemus was puzzled, wondering out loud how one could enter his mother's womb and be born again. To make sure Nicodemus didn't miss the importance of the words, Jesus repeats them in verse 7 in the form of a command: "Do not be amazed that I said to you, 'You must be born again.'"

The second question is "How will we be born again?" In verse 6, Jesus answers this by saying: "That which is born of the flesh is flesh, and that which is born of the Spirit is spirit." Nicodemus may have been wondering "What was wrong with the first womb and birth experience?" He assumed that all Jewish children were children of God because they were born to Jewish parents. Jesus said the first birth was inadequate to prepare anyone for entrance into His kingdom. Why? Nicodemus was certainly an upright citizen. Coming to Jesus to find out more information was certainly the right thing for him to do. We don't hear anything further about Nicodemus until the death of Jesus; he was one of those assisting with the burial of Jesus.[2]

---

[1] Romans 3:24
[2] John 19:39

The book of Romans spells out how God views the human race and makes it clear why it is absolutely necessary to be born again. We have already reviewed Romans 3:23 and 6:23, which reveal God's view of all human beings living on the face of the earth. Here they are again:

> All have sinned and fall short of the glory of God. (Romans 3:23)

> The wages of sin is death... (Romans 6:23)

That's pretty serious stuff! Every man, woman and child who come into this world by means of a mother's womb have this terminal sin disease thanks to Adam and Eve. David knew about it and wrote this:

> For I was born a sinner—yes, from the moment my mother conceived me.[3]

Happily, Romans 5:8 and 9 tell us more about the nature of God and the way of escape from our inherent nature that makes sin very tempting and our power to resist minimal. The Apostle Paul wrote to the Roman Christians and said:

> But God demonstrates His own love toward us, in that, while we were yet sinners, Christ died for us. Much more then, having now been justified [declared righteous] by His blood [that is, His death], we shall be saved from the wrath of God through Him.

This verse concludes with a tremendous beacon of hope, "but the free gift of God is eternal life in Christ Jesus our Lord."

A day of judgment is coming and that day is called "the day of God's wrath." Persons without Christ as their Advocate[4] will find his or her state of spiritual insensibilities made permanent. At that point there is no further possibility of salvation. "Today is the day of salvation," we read in Hebrews.[5] It is sad that individuals pass over this amazing gift from God and, by neglect, choose spiritual death. That is an eternal tragedy!

To the objection that God is a God of love and therefore would never show Himself to be an angry God, the response to that objection is easy, but

---

[3] Psalm 51:5 NLT

[4] 1 John 2:1; advocate, a person who argues for the cause of another person in a court of law (Merriam-Webster)

[5] Hebrews 3:13

sad. Just read the books of Jeremiah, Ezekiel, Hosea, or Joel. These books are not just books for another age and another people. They are the Word of God that also explain who God is. The tenderness of God is found in those books, but like a parent, His heart aches because of the punishment He must inflict first on Israel and later on Judah. The passages that show His wrath are hard to read, especially since they have a contemporary feel to them.

Since God went to great lengths to provide "the world" with the incredible gift of eternal life, a radical change for the better is now possible during this life. After death when the sinner stands before God in the Day of Judgment, he or she will have nothing to say but to admit they refused God's remedy for their terminal disease.

Nor do they have an advocate to plead their case. They will argue the merits of their good works, but Ephesians 2:8-9 is clear on that matter. Salvation (regeneration, sanctification, and glorification) is "not of works lest anyone should boast." There is no second chance according to Jesus' teachings and the only defense Christians may plead is the merits of Jesus Christ. There is little doubt that Satan will be standing by to claim his own. Job Chapters 1 and 2 make that clear.

This is also clear: the Scripture is talking about the permanent death of a sinner's spirit which is already dead during one's physical life unless the sinner has been the recipient of spiritual life by means of conversion. Permanent death or eternal death means total separation from God forever.[6] That's a greater separation than an unbeliever experiences in this life because during this life, God "causes His sun to rise on the evil and the good, and sends rain on the righteous and the unrighteous".[7]

Everlasting death for unrepentant sinners is a horrible end for those who have determined to remain in their sin during their lifetime on earth. But God sees that as justice. To defy God and live without a relationship with Him when He has provided the cure for sin at a terrible cost is a horrific way to pass into eternity. The Father still hears the crowd crying out, "Crucify Him! Crucify Him!" No father could ever forget that traumatic event especially when the event had a grand purpose: their salvation and salvation for all the rest of the world for all time! Sinners in every age are part of that crowd that shouted, "Crucify Him!"

---

[6] Compare Revelation 20:10 with Revelation 20:15 and Matthew 8:12
[7] Matthew 5:45

God is a great God who loves and He also exercises much patience, but His love has boundaries and His patience has limits; read the writings of the prophets who reveal what the limits are. Disregarding boundaries God has set has serious consequences.

III

What does it mean to be born again?

Sin entered the world because of Adam and Eve's disobedience. Do you remember that God said to them if they ate of the forbidden fruit, they would die? They did eat, and they did die, first spiritually, then physically. Expelled from the Garden of Eden made dying a reality.

Regeneration makes the spirit alive once again with functioning spiritual senses (all five are recorded in the Bible). A third part of one's being, the spirit, suddenly comes alive! A wonderful and awesome relationship is established with the Heavenly Father.

The life that is discussed here is God's kind of life infused in us at conversion by the Holy Spirit. It is like Adam's creation when God "breathed into his nostrils the breath of life." Alive in the spirit means fellowship with God. The Apostle Paul touches on the death of Adam as a result of his disobedience in eating of the fruit, "For as in Adam all die, so also in Christ all will be made alive."

What else does it mean to be regenerated or born again? The Scriptures say:

➢ It means, "But as many as received Him [Jesus], to them He gave the right to become children of God, even to those who believe in His name." John 1:12
➢ It means, "The Spirit Himself testifies with our spirit that we are children of God." -Romans 8:16
➢ It means, "See how great a love the Father has bestowed on us, that we would be called children of God; and such we are." - 1 John 3:1
➢ It means, "All of you who were baptized into Christ have clothed yourselves with Christ." -Galatians 3:27

Let me stop here to make sure you understand. If you did a gracious thing for me, I might respond, "Thank you. You're a saint." Humble Christians generally react to the use of the word saint. They will say, "You're welcome. I was glad to do it. But I'm not a saint." Really? Being called a "holy person" also evokes protests: "I'm still a sinner; I can't be a holy person!" The Bible says otherwise. Here are other examples:

➢ In Acts 26 while speaking to Agrippa, Paul gave his personal testimony and in doing so, referred to believers as saints:[8]

> And this is just what I did in Jerusalem; not only did I lock
> up many of the saints in prisons, having received authority
> from the chief priests, but also when they were being put
> to death I cast my vote against them.

➢ In Romans 16:15 Paul sends his greetings to five individuals in particular, and concludes with these words, "and [to] all the saints who are with them."

➢ Paul writes to the Corinthians in his second epistle (13:13), "All the saints greet you." He concludes his letter to the Philippian church similarly.

Does accepting such a compliment smack of pride and make you feel like a hypocrite? Probably it does because the term is linked in our minds to perfection. A usual comment is, "No, I'm not a saint because I'm not perfect." True, we are not perfect, but since Christians are not labeled as sinners once they are born again, what are they then? The Word of God says, "Saints"!

Yes, Christians are capable of sinning after they have been given the new nature but the new nature entitles them to be labeled saints, meaning holy persons. This is developed in the next chapter, salvation-sanctification. They may be immature like a baby who needs diaper changes, but they're still saints. The baby doesn't act like a person (a lot of training is necessary), but that baby is a person!

Don't minimize the work of God in your life nor forget the proper labeling of yourself as a saint. Don't erroneously call yourself a sinner and use that label as an excuse for non-growth. On the other hand, don't call yourself a saint and pat yourself on the back. The psalmist has written, "We are fearfully and wondrously made."[9] You are "somebody", as opposed to "junk" as a little boy once said of himself. The late Ethel Waters, African American blues and jazz singer, quoted the little boy, saying of himself, "I know I'm somebody 'cause God don't make no junk." No, He makes saints!

---

[8] Acts 26:10
[9] Psalm 138.14

Now, if you're a Christian, think of yourself as a saint, one whom God calls holy. Refrain from responding, "No, I'm not a saint, I'm just a sinner." That's not true. You are not a sinner like an unbeliever. It is more appropriate to say, "I'm a saint according to the Scriptures and no longer a slave to a sinful nature, but, yes, I can sin and I do sin for which I have the Lord's promise of forgiveness when I confess my sin." That's a long answer, but it is the right answer. 1 John 1:9 says:

> If we confess our sins, He is faithful and righteous to forgive
> us our sins and to cleanse us from all unrighteousness.

IV

How are we born again?

As to this question, "How are we born again?" The answer has to do with the Word of God. First Peter 1:23 says:

> You have been born again not of seed which is perishable
> but imperishable, that is, through the living and enduring
> word of God.

Another important word in explaining how we are born again is the verb "believe" (the noun form is "faith"). John 1:12 says that by believing, we are given the right to be called children of God. The verse is clear about the "how," "even to those who believe on His [Jesus'] name." John 3:16 tells us that whoever believes in Jesus receives the gift of eternal life.

What are we specifically asked to believe? Romans 10:9 gives us a clear answer: that we are to "confess with our mouth Jesus as Lord, and believe in our heart that God raised Him from the dead." The word "confess", in the original language (Greek), means "to say the same thing as another" and in this case, we are "to say the same thing God says about Jesus," that is, Jesus is Lord, and is alive, not dead.

To go this route means we first must acknowledge and confess we are sinners and need a Savior because the penalty of sin is eternal damnation. Jesus died to save sinners. To acknowledge the Son and His work is to acknowledge the Father and His plan.

Are you a believer in Jesus? Do you believe He died to pay the penalty for your sins? He did of course, and when you believe that truth, God accepts you as a Christian.[10] God gives you eternal life now… in this life. Upon realizing that is true, perhaps you might repeat Nicodemus' question, "How can these things be?"

In John 3:16, a verse beloved by many, Jesus explains the answer. Be sure you grasp the intent of the verb tense in that verse. As has been already pointed out, the word "have" is present tense, not "will have" but simply "have." And so is the verb "believe": "…whoever believes in Him [Jesus] shall not perish, but have eternal life." That's present tense.

A kernel of corn enables us to understand how this is so. Visualize a dried kernel of corn. Now describe it for me. You will probably say, "It is small, yellow, hard, and looks quite dead." Correct. But is it dead? And you would have to answer, "When the dead-looking kernel of corn is put into the ground, watered and warmed by the sun, it springs to life, grows into a stalk with green leaves, many times larger than the kernel, and is soft to the touch. It looks nothing like the kernel of corn that was put into the ground." How does that happen? The germ of life was in it before it was put into the ground and that germ of life transformed it.

Just so, Christian believer, you have within you the "germ of everlasting life" even though it is not evident on the outside in the here-and-now. Your present life will terminate in physical death and when that occurs, your body will be committed to the ground, but the real you is your soul and spirit and they are released at death to go to be with the Lord. A new body will be received at glorification.

In Ephesians 2, we reviewed verses 8 and 9; but go on to verse 10 where the Apostle Paul answers this particular question. Here are all three verses for context:

> For by grace you have been saved through faith; and that not
> of yourselves, it is the gift of God; not as a result of works, so
> that no one may boast. For we are His workmanship, created
> in Christ Jesus for [for the purpose of] good works, which
> God prepared beforehand so that we would walk in them.

These "good works" do not earn us regeneration, sanctification, or glorification. They are simply what we do in response to the love God has shown us in giving His Son to redeem us. Note that God has already prepared a package of good works for each of us.

The present tense of salvation-sanctification—the "being saved" aspect—is presented in the next chapter.

---

[10] John 1:12

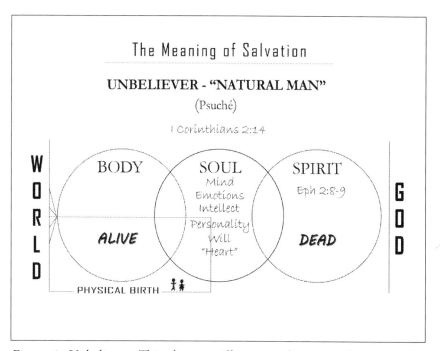

Figure 1. Unbeliever. This diagram illustrates the unsaved person. The unbeliever is born of father and mother (physical birth) and as a result, the body and soul are alive (see left and center circles); however, the spirit (see right circle) is dead.

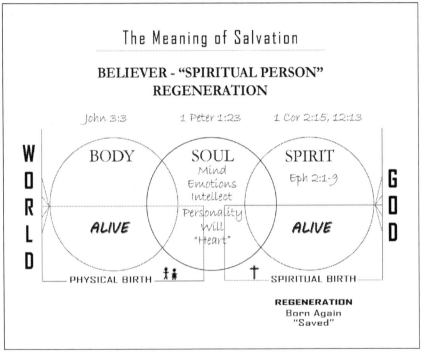

Figure 2. Believer. This diagram illustrates the believer. The believer is born of the Spirit (born again). This represents the second birth and the act of regeneration.

CHAPTER 6

SAVED FROM SELF!

Growing Up Christian

I

Have you ever acknowledged that you were a sinner, thanked God for His gift of His Son Jesus who died for your sins, and invited Jesus Christ into your life as your Savior and Lord? If you have done this, the Word of the God declares you are saved.[1] You are born again, regenerated! You are a Christian!

If you have been obedient to the Lord and "repented",[2] you have experienced the regeneration (born again) phase of salvation. You have taken that first step into a glorious relationship with God. You received God's gift of everlasting life at that moment of conversion according to John 3:16 (and explained in the previous chapter). That verse ends with these words, "... whoever believes in Him (Jesus) shall not perish but have everlasting life." God welcomes you into His family and He declares you to be His child.[3]

Are you aware there are old behaviors still hanging on, behaviors of your old life that now make you feel guilty and puzzled? Do you still experience bursts of anger, thoughts that are not consistent with Bible truths, and/or rough relationships with others? If you are "saved," why are there evidences of the old life still around?

---

[1] Romans 10:9-10

[2] To repent means to turn from one's old way of living to follow Christ; "repent" was John the Baptist's and Jesus' first message

[3] John 1:12

Perhaps you thought your old nature would be obliterated at your conversion. It was not. The old nature is still present, but—here is the big difference—it is no longer the ruling force in a Christian's life. When you invited Jesus to be Lord of your life, you not only received the gift of everlasting life but, you also received the gift of the Holy Spirit. It is the indwelling Holy Spirit who convicts of behavior that is inconsistent with the new life in Christ, and also who stands ready to give any Christian the power to deal with issues of the old life.

Jesus said the Holy Spirit would guide believers into all truth[4] so that one may "walk as Jesus walked."[5] Christians receive their guidance primarily through reading the Word of God and meditating on it. To be led by one's feelings is like being lost in a dense woods without a compass and deciding to go in a particular direction because it feels right. Christians, who know the Word of God, can resist the devil when he comes to tempt them to sin, and he will flee from them.[6] That is possible because of the power of the Spirit living within. The Apostle John reminds us, "Greater is He who is within you than he who is in the world."[7]

It is important that Christians understand what happens after their born again experience. If you have received Christ as your Savior and Lord, you can look back on that date and say, "That's the day I was saved." Technically, however, that is not the date you were saved but the day you were born again (regenerated) which is the first part of the God's plan of salvation.

Godly people tend to ask the question, "When were you saved?" What they want to know is "When were you born again?" There is a difference because there is more to salvation than regeneration. The use of the word saved, when it stands for a part of a whole is acceptable, but in this case, it is confusing because new believers believe they received the whole when in fact they received only a part.

As noted, the first phase or aspect is salvation-regeneration. But there is a second aspect of salvation that follows; it is referred to in Scripture as sanctification or holiness. To distinguish it from salvation-regeneration, I will refer to it as salvation-sanctification because it is also part of the plan of salvation—the second of three parts. It is the becoming-holy-in-thought-and-deed aspect of

---

[4] John 16:13
[5] 1 John 2:6
[6] James 4:7, Submit therefore to God. Resist the devil and he will flee from you.
[7] 1 John 4:4

our salvation. Regeneration is birth; sanctification is growth. Christians are "biblically illiterate" George Barna says, and the deficiency relates not to birth but to lack of growth. It is a sanctification problem.

For the Christian, regeneration is an act that has already occurred; it can be viewed as a past tense event. Sanctification, like growth, is a process with a starting point. It can also be viewed as a series of ongoing present tense events. Glorification is the grand finale event, the third aspect of salvation that Christians will experience in the future.

II

When Christians learn that a behavior they are engaged in is contrary to the will and purpose of God, they must learn how to overcome such behaviors. It usually comes as a shock to a new believer that the old nature still exists after repentance. Yes, the old nature still exists but as a believer there is a strong desire to want the new nature to succeed. However, there will be conflict between the two natures and the Christian, as the Apostle Paul discovered, the struggle may leave one feeling wretched.[8]

Sanctification is the process whereby a believer can overcome sinful behaviors. It is the work of the Holy Spirit to point out right from wrong, teaching believers what "sin, righteousness and judgment"[9] means from God's perspective. The battle may leave one feeling wretched, but when a habit is conquered, there is a feeling of great joy. One's conscience must agree with the Holy Spirit, but that "bad boy," the old nature, puts his nose in and loudly demands his way. The Holy Spirit is faithful; He will persist.

> But the Helper, the Holy Spirit, whom the Father will send
> in My name, He will teach you all things, and bring to your
> remembrance all that I said to you.[10]

Christians must welcome the Spirit's insistence that they come back in line with God's truth. Christians who profess to love God with all their hearts will appreciate the Spirit's pressure to bring them back in line. After confession is made, peace then floods the soul.

---

[8] Romans 7:24
[9] John 16:8
[10] John 14:26

The Spirit generally speaks by using the Word of God and that's why knowing the Word is so important. He convicts when there is inappropriate behavior; He then gives both wisdom and strength to the erring Christian to follow through. The deepest and most unsavory habits can be changed. How is this possible?

Let me make it personal. Take sarcasm for an example. Every time I was convicted of this behavior that is inappropriate and unbecoming a Christian, I had to confess my sin to the Lord. Each time I confessed was like inviting an ant to come and drop a grain of sand in a rut in the road. The process was slow (the habit was ingrained) and had to be repeated over and over. I must have patience. I know the Lord was having patience with me.

Eventually, those little tiny bits of sand began filling the rut. Do I still have to guard against that habit? Yes, but it is not the problem that it once was. Was that process humbling? You bet it was. The process was not only humbling but to be more honest, humiliating. Although I don't fall into that rut much anymore, I still have to be careful that the devil doesn't tempt me to go that way again. But see what the Word says about humbling one's self. James wrote, "Humble yourselves in the presence of the Lord, and He will exalt you."[11] Peter includes it in a list of values that are important for every believer, "To sum up, all of you be harmonious, sympathetic, brotherly, kindhearted, and humble in spirit."[12] In time, my troubling behavior was restrained and a habit of kindness (part of the fruit of the Spirit) began to take its place.

A Christian mother who has raised six children, now all married, may look in a mirror and, seeing her gray hairs, say with a smile, "I've earned every one of them!" She may conclude, "After raising six children, I've surely reached the pinnacle of patience by now!" I have news for this lady: "No, you haven't!" God will allow additional challenges no matter what one's situation or age. We will always be challenged and encouraged for further growth. Dear lady, the next challenge will probably involve your grandchildren! (This example is hypothetical.)

The Christian can depend on the Holy Spirit to show that the pinnacle is higher still! The top would be perfection and we will not experience perfection until the Lord receives us to Himself. He will help us take another step toward the ultimate pinnacle each day while on earth and He will produce His fruit

---

[11] James 4:10
[12] 1 Peter 3:8

within us (godly patience along with the rest of the fruit of the Spirit: love, joy, peace, kindness, goodness, faithfulness, gentleness, and self-control).[13] The Holy Spirit will help shape our behavior until it becomes more like that of Christ's behavior.

Becoming holy entails a life-long process because the Christian will be constantly confronted with new events and generally an array of new people of all kinds of personalities. Some of these events and some of these people will require a new level of humility and kindness.

> SANCTIFICATION has to do with how
> a Christian reacts and responds.
> Reaching for a new level of kindness
> is to be perfecting holiness.

Others will marvel at the patience a Christian-saint exercises, saying, "I don't know how you are able to resist lashing back!" They will admit that the patience they have been witnessing is beyond anything they have ever seen. That is because it is a display of Holy Spirit-inspired patience. That's good news. That's a great testimony because it demonstrates before others what Jesus is like. On the other hand, Barna's findings seem to be saying that contemporary Christians are not only like the world, but they seem to be stuck in the world's culture

In the New Testament, the writer of the book of Hebrews and the Apostle Peter both speak of the absolute necessity of a believer becoming sanctified, that is, manifesting a life of holiness. Hebrews 12:14 says this about holiness, "Make every effort to live in peace with all men and to be holy; without holiness no one will see the Lord." Let me repeat that last phrase: "without holiness no one will see the Lord." What we are talking about in this chapter is to be put at the top of every Christian's agenda.

Peter, remembering Old Testament truths, wrote in his first epistle, "But just as he who called you is holy [that's God], so be holy in all you do; for he himself [that's God] has said, 'You must be holy because I am holy.'"[15] Read

---

[13] Galatians 5:22-23
[14] Second Corinthians 7:1
[15] 1 Peter 1:15-16 (NIV)

that verse again. Don't slide over that powerful word "must" too quickly. Holiness is not optional!

So the essential question is "who are you?" Are you a child of God? That which identifies Christians as children of God is holiness. Think of an immigration official who demands to see your identification when you wish to enter his country. You present your passport, which tells the agent, unequivocally, that you are an American. The agent authenticates your identity and welcomes you into his country.

Picture a mountain called Mount Holiness and picture a Christian beginning to climb that mountain. It will be a difficult climb, but the Holy Spirit is just above always ready to throw down a rope. He is strong enough to pull the climber who grabs the rope to the next level.

As a child grows up to be like his or her father, so are we to grow up spiritually and become like our heavenly Father who is basically, in his nature, holy. In Him no sin will ever be found and that is what He expects of us. The Christian's transformed nature who, at regeneration, is declared to be holy now has the responsibility, ability, and help to become holy.

There is a great need for evangelists but their messages are inappropriate in a church setting, or put another way, "they are preaching to the choir" when they are preaching to an assembly of saints. When the church gathers together, it is for edification. As to the evangelists, "Go to the street corners and invite to the banquet anyone you find." And, "Go into all the world and proclaim the gospel to the whole creation."[16] "Believers gather for edification and scatter for evangelism." That's what Richard C. Halverson, the late chaplain of the United States Senate, once said. He had it right! Many churches haven't yet learned this valuable truth! If a church board desires to wake up a sleepy church, don't call evangelists! Call Bible teachers!

While attending the local university full time after our international service abroad, a local church asked if I would fill their pulpit. Their pastor of many years had just retired and they were down to a dozen people who were planning to close the doors in a month or so. The twelve congregants were all over 60 except one lady who was in her fifties.

Two things I found important in revitalizing this congregation: lots of love and teaching the "meat and potatoes" of the Word of God. I prepared detailed sermon notes and notes to read Monday through Friday preparing for the next Sunday. In a year, 12 became 50 and in three years, the small

---

[16] Matthew 22:9 (NLT). 28:19 (ESV)

chapel was full: 160! At one point, we doubled from 50 to 100 in two weeks' time thanks to an influx of former hippies who had found the Lord through the faithful service of a single obedient Christian. That evangelist then sought out a church fellowship where these new believers would be welcomed and trained in the Word. There were no children for the nursery or Sunday School until the number suddenly reached 100. Then the number went from zero to 27 in the toddlers' nursery!

These new congregants, mostly young couples, were already saved. They didn't need salvation messages (i.e., the necessity to be born-again messages). They needed "meat and potato" messages.

To accomplish the Great Commission, every believer has some responsibility to check out "the street corners" or "main highways" (as another translation has it), as well as the whole of creation. Our evangelist mentioned above was actually a student of the Word and he attempted to teach all these new believers with all their children in a home. When he realized it was too much for him, he went church shopping to find a church where these newcomers to the faith could be mentored properly and accepted in their bare feet and paint overalls.

Our evangelist reminded me of Paul's Timothy. Paul wrote to Timothy and said:

> But you, be sober in all things, endure hardship, do the work
> of an evangelist, fulfill your ministry.[17]

Maturing is the second aspect of salvation, that is, salvation-sanctification. Christians at this stage in their journey need the exegesis of biblical texts. They are not only ready for a clear explanation of the Word of God but also for practical application of the truths that are being taught.
Compare these two verses:

➢ 1 Peter 2:2 - ...like newborn babies, long for the pure milk of the word, so that by it you may grow in respect to salvation...

➢ Hebrew 5:12-13 - For though by this time you ought to be teachers, you have need again for someone to teach you the elementary principles of the oracles of God, and you have come to need milk and not solid food. For everyone who partakes only of milk is not accustomed to the word of righteousness, for he is an infant.

---

[17] 2 Timothy 4:5

NIV translates the phrase "word of righteousness" this way, "the teaching about righteousness." The New Living Translation presents the entire verse this way, "For someone who lives on milk is still an infant and doesn't know how to do what is right."

The texts say milk is for "newborn babies" and "infants," and for those who are not accustomed to the "word (or, teaching) of righteousness." The author of Hebrews ties "babes" and "infants" to elementary principles and ties "the word (or, teaching) of righteousness" to solid food. Christians need to know what is right and what is wrong in their new life in Christ and that requires "solid food" and "solid food" is the "meat and potatoes" of the Word. It is intentionally something more substantial than "milk."

The Apostle Paul was very excited about what he was going to learn next. What was Paul expecting to see or hear? Paul shared this with the Corinthian church and you will get a feel for what he was expecting the Holy Spirit to reveal.[18]

> But we speak God's wisdom in a mystery, the hidden wisdom which God predestined before the ages to our glory; the wisdom which none of the rulers of this age has understood; for if they had understood it they would not have crucified the Lord of glory;
>
> But just as it is written,
>
> Things which eye has not seen, and ear has not heard, and which have not entered the heart or man, all that God has prepared for those who love Him."[19]
>
> For to us God revealed them through the Spirit; for the Spirit searches all things, even the depths of God.
>
> For who among men knows the thoughts of a man except the spirit of the man which is in him? Even so the thoughts of God no one knows except the Spirit of God.
>
> Now we have received, not the spirit of the world, but the Spirit who is from God, so that we may know the things freely given to us by God.

---

[18] 1 Corinthians 2:7-12

[19] 1 Corinthians 2:9, is quoted from Isaiah 64:4 but not a verbatim quote

III

Shouldn't the church be concerned about unbelievers? Of course! Shouldn't the church's services be made more attractive and livelier to draw in unbelievers? If it surprises you when I say the answer is no, then you need to study the word church as Scripture describes and defines it.

The biblical definition of the word church is "an assembly of believers" rather than "a building" as Webster's dictionary first defines it. In 1 Corinthians 14, the church is described as a group of believers who come together for edification. When a church (the assembly of believers) gathers together it is for the "meat and potatoes" of the Word, not for evangelism or even for the milk of the Word.[20]

You may ask, "Shouldn't we encourage unbelievers to come to our worship services?" This is my answer: Only if you have witnessed to them and they have begun to respond to your witness. Otherwise, they are not ready for the "meat and potatoes" of the Word. If the early church was anything like the church in West Africa where my wife and I served as international workers in the mid-twentieth century, nobody entered the space the church set aside for their meetings unless they were ready to convert.

But what if there is an unbeliever present? Paul addresses that possibility in 1 Corinthians 14. He wrote, "But if all prophesy, and an unbeliever or an ungifted man enters, he is convicted by all, he is called to account by all."[21] Prophecy is speaking forth the Word and sharing an application. Vine's Dictionary of New Testament Words gives as the first meaning for the word prophecy this definition: "telling forth the Divine counsels." The second meaning is "foretelling."

Early churches did not have the canon of Scripture as we have today. They had the words of Jesus as shared by the Apostles, and had copies of, or at least knowledge of the Old Testament. Eventually, they had copies of the letters written by John, Paul, Jude, and Peter. The Holy Spirit, as Jesus promised, would guide them and give them insights concerning divine truth.

A believer in the Corinthian church might have raised his or her hand, be recognized, and say, "I have an insight about that issue we are discussing based on something I learned from the Mosaic law. If it correlates with the

---

[20] See 1 Corinthians 14
[21] 1 Corinthians 14:24

law of love that Jesus taught—and I believe it does—then I think we have the answer for that issue."

Shouldn't newborn adult Christians be fed milk? Of course, but it is certainly advisable to have special classes for them to bring them up to speed so they can begin to appreciate solid food. If the foundation of elementary principles is laid, those once regenerated with new life in Christ will be hungry to know the Word. They are ready to ask questions at the youngster stage. Do you remember the why's and "What are you doing?" of that stage?

Where in the average evangelical church programming do they have that opportunity? Who will answer their questions? Shouldn't a mentor be appointed to assist new believer's transition into their new life? There are many who have come forward to an altar to confess their need of Christ as Lord and Savior. Then what? How many have been mentored? How many are walking with Jesus a year later?

That may well be significant reason newer believers, especially younger people, quit attending evangelical churches. If they have been born again but only milk is offered they will be turned off. Up-tempo music will attract them, but only expositional teaching and its application of the Word of God will hold them and prepare them to serve Christ. (Remember also to include the love dimension because teaching without it is called *a lecture*.)

Their faith must be anchored first! Then in a setting of edification, they can hear the persuasive voice of the Spirit calling them to serve in ministries of their own. When they find purpose and usefulness, they will serve God effectively and joyfully. Do you see the signs Boomers are holding up (figuratively speaking)? These signs proclaim:

> "In-Depth Teaching Wanted!"

> "Are the Scriptures Relevant for the 21st Century?"

> "How Can Boomers, Busters, and Millennials Apply Biblical Truth?"

Alas, the structure promoted by the Builders generation to compensate for the loss of the Sunday evening evangelistic hour promotes evangelism at the expense of edification. I believe Boomers want to be taught how to experience the presence of God. They need spiritual edification so they can handle today's knotty, nasty and nearly unsolvable problems. They need godly mentors. The Bible has answers about how to live in a rotting world. Unfortunately, church leaders are not reading the signs nor sending out *alerts* to their congregations.

Calling pastor-teachers to a local church and putting pressure on them to be evangelists is a problem that needs to be addressed. Statistics at the close of the year appear to be more important in judging the effectiveness of the pastor as an evangelist than whether the congregation is maturing in love and in the knowledge of holiness.

The popularity of books like Brother Lawrence's *Practicing the Presence of God*, A. W. Tozer's *The Pursuit of God* and *The Knowledge of the Holy*, Henry Blackaby's *Experiencing God: Knowing and Doing the Will of God,* and others of the same genre should tell pastor-teachers something about the hunger of God's people! There are many Boomers who are hungry not only for the truth of the Word of God but also for understanding how to apply the truth. They don't see much application in the Christian community.

To the degree that Christians demonstrate purity in their lives reflecting Christlike behavior, to that degree, they glorify God and to that degree they are perfecting holiness. Sanctification is growing up, that is, maturing spiritually as a Christian. It requires a decision of the mind to turn everything—I repeat, *everything*—over to the Lord,[22] followed by multiple godly decisions throughout the rest of one's life.[23]

Again, this relates to Romans Chapter 12:1-2 which we will examine at the end of this chapter.

IV

Salvation-sanctification ought to be a priority. The answers to the following three questions are some of the "meat and potatoes" of the Faith.

1. What Does Sanctification Mean?

2. How Does Sanctification Occur?

3. When Does Sanctification Occur?

The regenerated individual has been birthed as a full-fledged Christian whose spirit, once dead in trespasses and sins,[24] is now alive with spiritual

---

[22] Roman 12:1
[23] Romans 12:2
[24] See Ephesians 2

senses functioning: hearing, seeing, tasting,[25] touching,[26] and smelling (aroma).[27] We know babies need milk to grow and so do new Christians whom Scriptures describe as "babes." We also know a baby is switched from milk to baby food, and then to "meat and potatoes" as he or she grows. So also, brand new Christians who, after digesting the milk of the Word, need solid food.

The "meat and potatoes" of the Word consist of the deeper truths that the Apostle Paul spoke about when writing to the Corinthian church. He wrote:

> The wisdom we speak of is the mystery of God—his plan that was previously hidden, even though he made it for our ultimate glory before the world began... For to us God revealed them through the Spirit; for the Spirit searches all things, even the depths of God.[28]

And that brings us back to sanctification.

What Does Sanctification Mean?

In discussing sanctification, we need to understand the meaning of the word as well as the meaning of the related word holiness.

- ➤ Greek usage of the word sanctification.
  - • Thayer's Lexicon: *hagiasmos* means consecration, purification; also the effect of consecration

- ➤ The verb is *hagiazo* and is translated:
  - • to be holy, to be a holy person, to be a saint
  - • to be sanctified, to sanctify
  - • theologically: to be separated from sin and devoted to God

- ➤ Vincent's Word Studies on *hagiasmos* agrees and notes that "it is translated *holiness* in the AV of Rom 6:19, 22; 1Th 4:7; 1Ti 2:15; Hebrews 12:14 but is always rendered "sanctification" in the RV" and adds a word about the noun:

---

[25] Psalm 34:8

[26] 1 John 1:1

[27] 2 Corinthians 2:16 and Philippians 4:8. The International Standard Bible Encyclopedia states: "Acceptable sacrifices and pious conduct are called a "sweet smell" or "savor" (Exodus 29:18; Ephesians 5:2; Philippians 4:18) "well-pleasing to God."

[28] 1 Corinthians 1:7, 10 (NLT)

- *hagiasmos* signifies separation to God, 1 Cor. 1:30; 1 Peter 1:2
- *hagiasmos* can also indicate the resultant state, the conduct befitting those so separated, 1 Thessalonians 4:3,4, and 7.

How Does Sanctification Occur?

➢ The Apostle Paul wrote about sanctification in his letters to the churches:

- Romans 6:19 – "…so now present your members as slaves to righteousness, resulting in sanctification."

- Romans 6:22 – "But now having been freed from sin and enslaved to God, you derive your benefit, resulting in sanctification, and the outcome, eternal life."

- 1 Thessalonians 4:3 – "For this is the will of God, your sanctification; that is, that you abstain from sexual immorality…"[29]

- 2 Thessalonians 2:13 – "But we should always give thanks to God for you, brethren beloved by the Lord, because God has chosen you from the beginning for salvation through sanctification by the Spirit and faith in the truth."

➢ The command, "Be holy," is found addressed to Israel in Leviticus 11:44-45; 19:2; and 20:7; Jehovah (Yahweh) saw those with whom He entered into a covenant as His children according to Psalm 103:13, "Just as a father has compassion on his children, so the Lord has compassion on those who fear Him." New Testament believers are also spoken of as the children of God.[30] To be the children of a Father who is by nature holy, assumes the children are also holy. Holy is the norm, the natural thing to be; not to be holy is not to be a child of God.

---

[29] "sexual immorality" — the Greek word probably includes unions of any kind that the Word of God prohibits
[30] Matthew 5:45; Luke 6:35; Romans 8:16, 17; 1 John 3:2

> VINCENT DEFINES SANCTIFICATION
> Sanctification is thus the state predetermined by
> God for believers, into which in grace He calls
> them, and in which they begin their Christian
> course… Sanctification is that relationship with
> God into which men enter by faith in Christ and
> to which their sole title is the death of Christ.

A Christian is to be chaste and modest, pure from faults, clean and free from blemishes, that is, from moral stains in mind and behavior. Being holy is the Christian's "calling" and it is explained quite simply yet forthrightly in 1 Thessalonians 4:7 (NIV), "For God did not call us to be impure, but to live a holy life." Therefore, this is what we should be addressing daily.

The most unusual aspect of sanctification/holiness—something we rarely stop to think about—is the fact this high view of a moral God is not known elsewhere in the world nor is it known in any other religious system. We should not be surprised. It could not be known elsewhere because its origin had to be a revelation from God Himself.

It is not found in human DNA. When humans experience the new birth, they are transformed into a new person and the Holy Spirit enables Christians to have a spiritual DNA. Paul assured the Corinthians of such a transformation, "Therefore, if anyone is in Christ, the new creation has come: The old has gone, the new is here!"[31] The New Living Translation says, "Anyone who belongs to Christ has become a new person. The old life is gone; a new life has begun!"

Scriptures tell us that it is Christ to whom we are indebted for sanctification, 1 Corinthians 1:30 says: But by His [God's] doing you are in Christ Jesus, who became to us wisdom from God, and righteousness and sanctification, and redemption. To embrace Christ, is to embrace wisdom, righteousness, sanctification and redemption. What a privilege! What a blessing! Vincent says this:

> ➢ Sanctification must be learned from God.
>   • 1 Thessalonians. 4:4, as He teaches it by His Word, John 17:17, 19; cp. Psalm 17:4; 119:9

---

[31] 2 Corinthians 5:17 (NIV)

- • Sanctification must be pursued by the believer, earnestly, and undeviatingly.
- • 1 Timothy 2:15; Hebrews 12:14

➢ Sanctification cannot be transferred or imputed (the holy character is not vicarious); it is an individual possession, built up, little by little, a result of obedience to the Word of God, and following the example of Christ in the power of the Holy Spirit.
- • 1 Thessalonians 3:13
- • Matthew 11:29; John 13:15; Ephesians 4:20; Philippians 2:5; Romans 8:13; Ephesians 3:16

SANCTIFICATION

is

taught by God

pursued by the believer

not transferable to another.

In the Old Testament, the key to holiness can be summed up in one word—the same word that sums up holiness in the New Testament for Christians: obedience. Jesus summed up the whole of the Old Testament laws succinctly when He taught that we are to love God with our entire being and love our neighbor as we love ourselves.[32]

In his day, the prophet Jeremiah clarified the Old Testament teaching on holiness in terms that avoided the legalism often associated (wrongly) with the Old Testament. He wrote this:

> Thus says the LORD of hosts, the God of Israel, ...I did not speak to your fathers, or command them in the day that I brought them out of the land of Egypt, concerning burnt offerings and sacrifices. But this is what I commanded them, saying, "Obey My voice, and I will be your God, and you will be My people; and you will walk in all the way which I command you, that it may be well with you." [33]

---

[32] Deuteronomy 6:5, Numbers 15:16; Matthew 19:19, 22:38-39
[33] Jeremiah 7:21-23

The path of obedience is the path to holiness. Holiness is not achieved through good works however good those works may be. Remember, we are not born into this new life (regenerated) by good works, and neither do we become holy (sanctified) by good works. That's all the work of God through the Holy Spirit. Our part? Hear the Word and yield to the Word: Obedience!

God told Abraham that blamelessness was imperative. In Genesis 17:1, God said, "Walk before Me, and be blameless." That's a command. Paul explains how Abraham pleased God. He said when he wrote his epistle to the church at Rome, "For what does the Scripture say? 'Abraham believed God, and it was credited to him as righteousness.'" [34] Abraham was a man of faith and that was the basis for his blamelessness.

Job—who probably preceded Abraham chronologically—had this testimony, "There was a man in the land of Uz whose name was Job; and that man was blameless." [35]

God says this about Job when speaking to Satan, "Have you considered My servant Job? For there is no one like him on the earth, a blameless and upright man, fearing God and turning away from evil." God called Job "blameless" and there is no better testimonial than that! Yes, it is possible for a human being, imperfect and prone to sinning, to be blameless. Job feared (reverenced) God and turned away from evil. That's an Old Testament definition of sanctification consistent with the New Testament.

David provides us with another clue in Psalm 19:13. He prays, "Keep back your servant from presumptuous sins; Let them not rule over me; Then I will be blameless, And I shall be acquitted of great transgression." The New Living Translation puts it this way, "Keep your servant from deliberate sins! Don't let them control me. Then I will be free of guilt and innocent of great sin."

The Greek word translated presumptuous or deliberate is defined by Gesenius in his Hebrew-Chaldee dictionary as "proud and connected with the idea of insolence and impiety." David recognizes this deadly sin and prays for God's help to keep him from it. When we are doing well with God's blessing, this sin of pride can rise up to take control of our hearts before we can even identify it. Prayers asking God's help are also a factor in learning to be blameless.

The Apostle Paul provides us with yet another clue. He wrote to the Philippian church these words:

---

[34] Romans 4:3
[35] Job 1:1

And this I pray, that your love may abound still more and more in real knowledge and all discernment, so that you may approve the things that are excellent, in order to be sincere and blameless until the day of Christ.[36]

He wrote to the Thessalonians in a similar vein:

May the Lord cause you to increase and abound in love for one another, and all people, just as we also do for you; so that He may establish your hearts without blame in holiness before our God and Father at the coming of our Lord Jesus with all His saints.[37]

The clue here is "that your love may abound still more and more." Loving one another is certainly an important consideration for the one looking forward to blamelessness!

In summary, we can see that David presented the negative in Psalm 19:13—what to stay away from while Paul presented the positive in his letters to the Philippians and Thessalonians—what to embrace.

When the Holy Spirit finds no sin in us, we are blameless at that point in our walk with the Lord. This does not mean that we won't sin again. Most probably we will. But at that moment in time, having confessed any known sin, a believer stands blameless before God.

Meditate on 2 Corinthians 7:1 that says this, "Therefore, having these promises, beloved, let us cleanse ourselves from all defilement of flesh and spirit, perfecting holiness in the fear of God.

How can it be that the Savoir will present us to the Father "blameless"? How can our holiness be perfected? Can imperfect people really demonstrate perfect holiness? And that, the Scriptures tell us, is precisely what He will do.

That would be scary except for an additional clue found in Peter's word about the suffering of Christians, and Jude's glorious benediction:

PETER — After you have suffered for a little while, the God of all grace, who called you to His eternal glory in Christ, will Himself perfect, confirm, strengthen and establish you.[38]

---

[36] Philippians 1:19
[37] 1 Thessalonians 3:12-13
[38] 1 Peter 5:10

JUDE - Now to Him who is able to keep you from stumbling, and to make you stand in the presence of His glory blameless with great joy, to the only God our Savior, through Jesus Christ our Lord, be glory, majesty, dominion and authority, before all time and now and forever. Amen.[39]

What is the clue? It is God's part in the perfection of our holiness. After we have suffered for a little while, the God of all grace Himself will perfect you! And, [He] is able to keep us from stumbling and to make us stand in His presence blameless! The very power and mercy of God insures that He will work with His children so that at the time of their presentation before Him, His children will be blameless. Even now, Christians are unaware that He keeps them from stumbling many times, but they will learn in Heaven how much busier He has been than they realize, busy watching over His family on earth.

I hear you saying, "I'm a Christian but I do stumble!" That is true, and so do I. But you are forgetting another wonderful truth about our great God: when we confess our sin, he forgives us of that sin, and remembers it against us no more forever![40] He doesn't keep a record of forgiven sin.

Both Paul and Peter speak of "the sanctifying work of the Holy Spirit". Paul wrote:

But we ought always to thank God for you, brothers loved by the Lord, because from the beginning God chose you to be saved through the sanctifying work of the Spirit and through belief in the truth.[41]

Peter wrote:

[We] have been chosen according to the foreknowledge of God the Father, through the sanctifying work of the Spirit, for obedience to Jesus Christ and sprinkling by blood.[42]

---

[39] Jude 24-25
[40] Hebrews 10:17
[41] 2 Thessalonians 2:13
[42] 1 Peter 1:2

How does God's plan for sanctification work?

Christ died to pay the penalty for your sin and every other sin you confess. Christ sent the Holy Spirit who performs *"the sanctifying work of the Spirit"*[43] God shows His mercy to forgive, exercising His power to never remember it forever!

PATH TO SANCTIFICATION
Struggle with right and wrong; choose wrong…
Conviction of the wrong choice (work of the Holy Spirit)…
Guilty conscience…
Loss of inner peace…
Confession (urged by the Holy Spirit)…
Cleansing of the guilty conscience (work of the Holy Spirit)…
Restoration of peace (result of work by the Holy Spirit)

When Does Sanctification Occur?

Romans 12:1 and 2 answer this question. Verse one is the starting point and verse two is what happens subsequently. This is Paul's testimony as well as the application of the theology outlined in the first eleven chapters of Romans. In those chapters, he talks, among other topics, about the pervasiveness of sin, the strength of faith, and the need for holiness. Do you remember the struggle he had in Chapter 7?

> For I know that nothing good dwells in me, that is, in my flesh; for the willing is present in me, but the doing of the good is not… on the one hand I myself with my mind am serving the law of God, but on the other, with my flesh the law of sin.[44]

Paul's answer to this dilemma? Continue reading into Chapter 8 and see his glorious answer in verses one and two:

---

[43] 1 Peter 1:2
[44] Romans 7:13, 25b

> Therefore there is now no condemnation for those who are in Christ Jesus. For the law of the Spirit of life in Christ Jesus has set you free from the law of sin and of death.[45]

Paul explains in more detail when writing to the Galatians:

> "I have been crucified with Christ; and it is no longer I who live, but Christ lives in me; the life which I now live in the flesh I live by faith in the Son of God, who loved me and gave Himself up for me."[46]

The question is this: how did Paul get from his experience in Romans seven and his victory statements in Romans eight and Galatians two? Paul explains the answer when he arrives at Romans 12:1-2. Chapter 12 begins the practical section of the book of Romans.

Incidentally, do you want to know the will of God for your life? To understand the text found in Romans 12:1-2 is to be privy to the will of God according to verse 2b. Here are verses one and two.

VERSE 1 - the appeal for sanctification

> Therefore I urge you, brethren, by the mercies of God, to present your bodies a living and holy sacrifice, acceptable to God, which is your spiritual service of worship.

➢ Paul now turns to application based on the first eleven chapters: note the word "therefore". Carl Westerlund in his commentary lists four therefores in Romans that indicate the four major themes:
  • The "therefore…" of condemnation, Romans 3:20
  • The "therefore…" of justification, Romans 5:1
  • The "therefore…" of sanctification, Romans 8:1
  • The "therefore…" of dedication, Romans 12:1

➢ Paul, seeing the importance of application, begins with a plea, *I urge you,* or, *I plead with you.*
  • Paul is addressing Christian believers: brethren

---

[45] Romans 8:1-2
[46] Galatians 2:20

- The grounds for Paul's appeal: the mercies of God; this is compassion Paul himself has experienced and the heart of a compassionate God who made known this wonderful plan of salvation to those who crucified His Son. We might say, "Because of the goodness the Lord has shown to you…" Paul then reveals how one becomes holy as God is holy.

- What Paul asks believers to do: present themselves. For the verb "present," Paul uses a Greek tense not found in English. It is called the aorist tense and is to be understood more for its action than timing. It is an action like taking a photograph that captures a view and that view is a slice of time. When the photo is taken, the action is completed. Paul is saying, "Present yourself once for all." He views it as a onetime action and that action results in opening one's self to the work of the Holy Spirit without reservations. This action of holding nothing back from the Spirit is not generally understood nor experienced by new Christians.

- Since these words indicate that Paul has a sacrifice in mind, NIV translates the word "present" as "offer". This describes one who would come to an altar to offer a sacrifice. The sacrifice in this case is your body (i.e., one's self). In Greek, the word body can be used to represent the whole man.

- Is this an action required of believers who have already experienced salvation-regeneration? Emphatically yes! It's addressed to "brethren," that is, Christians. This starts the believer on the journey of becoming what God has declared believers to be: holy. Without this step on the part of the believer, he or she cannot become holy or experience the strength and wisdom the Holy Spirit gives to become holy.

Since the action called for in verse one is full commitment or dedication without reservation, that means Paul is calling on believers to turn over to the Holy Spirit every thought of one's mind, every feeling of one's sensibilities including all emotions and all values one claims as one's own. The aorist verb tense

Paul uses here describes punctiliar action.[47] That once-and-for-all commitment invites the Holy Spirit to come in and start the work of sanctification.[48] What is involved here is opening the door to that part of one's being—the soul—so the Holy Spirit who already has access to the believer's spirit, can help the believer evaluate what is consistent with the will of God and what is not. Thus the Christian's body becomes a holy temple where God dwells.[49]

It's like inviting a guest into your home but he is left standing in the foyer of a home. What is needed is an invitation, giving him the right to step into the living space. If he has come to take possession of your home, then you must give him the key to the home and let him examine every room and closet in the house. This is what the Spirit desires to do but He won't examine every room and every closet unless you invite Him to do so.

This is what brought Paul from despair (Romans 7) to victory (Romans 8:1-2). We surely can believe that, at one point, Paul offered himself without reservation and then peace settled in and he began to understand the will of God for his life.

> ➤ Paul calls for Christians to make themselves a living sacrifice
>   • Our blood does not have to be shed, as was the blood of goats and bulls, since Christ gave Himself as our sacrifice and His blood was shed on our behalf. For men and women to be a living sacrifice is not a sacrifice for sin but rather a thanksgiving sacrifice.
> ➤ God is pleased with this offering of ourselves: wholly acceptable to God
>   • If you are a Christian and have not yet experienced the truth of Romans 12:1 and 2, listen carefully when you pray. You surely will hear the Spirit of the Lord encouraging you to place yourself on His altar as "a living sacrifice." Why is this difficult? It is because it means you must give up being lord

---

[47] The aorist tense is said to be "simple occurrence" or "summary occurrence", without regard for the amount of time taken to accomplish the action. This tense is often referred to as the "punctiliar tense" meaning a "one-point-in-time action." -- ntgreek. org/learn_nt_greek/verbs

[48] When these verses are not taught and understood by born-again Christians, they not only remain illiterate but will struggle with their faith. They will show little of the fruit of the Spirit although claiming to be Christian.

[49] 1 Corinthians 3:16-17 and 6:19

of your life and let Jesus be what you claimed He would be when you were born again, your Savior and Lord.

- At this point, you will begin to understand what God wants you to do with your life. I assure you, His plan for your life will be so much more beautiful than any plans you may have for your own life.

➢ This is the only worship that makes sense: This is your reasonable (rational) worship.

- It's reasonable in light of what God has done for everyone who comes to Him and receives the salvation He offers freely. In fact, we would be perfectly correct in saying it's more than reasonable! It's rational because our death—when we die to self-ambitions is more meaningful to God than the death of lambs and bulls. Dying to self is an act of love toward the God who first loved us.[50]

COMMITMENT TO SANCTIFICATION
Addressed to Christians as
an urgent matter: turn over self to God.
Romans 12:1

VERSE 2 - the sanctification lifestyle

> And do not be conformed to this world, but be transformed by the renewing of your mind, so that you may prove what the will of God is, that which is good and acceptable and perfect.

All the verbs in this verse are in the present tense in Greek, a tense that generally denotes continuous or habitual action. The verse can be understood as follows:

> Do not continue to be conformed to this world, but continue to be transformed by the continual renewing of your mind, so that you may continue to prove what the will of God is, that which is good and acceptable and perfect.[51]

---

[50] 1 John 4:19
[51] Romans 12:2

The verse is cumbersome translated in this fashion, but this is Paul's intent in light of the verb tenses he used. Sanctification, according to this verse, is very much a process, whereas verse one is the once-and-for-all commitment.

> ➤ The Christian's spiritual pattern for living the Christian life: do not continue to be conformed, but continue to be transformed. Do not fashion yourself after the world's pattern but be transformed according to the Lord's pattern as detailed in Scripture.
>   - Note the meaning of the word transformed in Greek is a recognizable word for English speakers: *metamorphoö*. According to Vine, this Greek word "refers to the permanent state to which a change takes place." Butterflies experience a metamorphosis when they go from a worm-like stage to a beautiful creature with wings.
>
>   - What will happen: a [continual] renewing. This renewing is refreshingly beautiful when the changes in a believer's personality are noticed. This is an ongoing process and will continue until we see Jesus.
>
>   - Where this change takes place: the mind. That's where all our values are stored and they govern our behavior. When the Spirit digs up a near forgotten sinful thought that needs to be confessed, the Christian's will is now addressed. The Spirit introduces conviction and the rest is up to the will of the believer. Sometimes we reject the Spirit's conviction and stay troubled, sometimes we try to stonewall the Spirit, and sometimes we confess[52] the sinful behavior and experience relief, then peace and joy.
>
>   - The result of this process is that one becomes more sanctified (more holy): that you may prove what is the good, and perfect and acceptable will of God.
>
>   - The Greek word used here for "prove" applies to metals and to the operation of testing or trying metals by fire to rid them of dross. Barnes adds, "It also means to explore, investigate, ascertain. This is its meaning here. The sense is, that such

---

[52] Confess in Greek is literally "to say the same thing another" or, "to agree with another"; in this case, one is agreeing with God and what He is saying about a Christian's particular behavior

a renewed mind is essential to a successful inquiry after the will of God. The heart that is renewed is best suited to appreciate and understand His will."[53]

•   To prove in this fashion allows the dross of what we are hearing from our culture to fall away and leave the pure gold and silver of the Word of God. That permits the Christian to discern what truly is "the good, perfect, and acceptable will of God." Christians don't need to speculate about the will of God! This is how one can know the will of God.

LIVING A SANCTIFIED LIFE
Don't use the world as a pattern; be transformed, resulting in the renewing of the mind and learning the will of God.
Romans 12:2

Peter wrote, "but like the Holy One who called you, be holy yourselves also in all your behavior." [54] Jesus told His disciples this, "By their fruits you shall know them."[55] Here's the fruit Paul said he would look for:

> Therefore I, the prisoner of the Lord, implore you to walk in a manner worthy of the calling with which you have been called[56] with all humility and gentleness, with patience, showing tolerance for one another in love, being diligent to preserve the unity of the Spirit in the bond of peace.[57]

Have we made that once-and-for-all commitment of all our values, all our behaviors, and especially all our will, as Romans 12:1 urges us to do? Are we growing in the grace and knowledge of our Lord because we are able to discern God's good, perfect, and acceptable will as per Romans 12:2?

How do you measure up? Can others tell the difference as they look at your behavior? They may say, "I've never met another person as kind as you." Quietly say, "Thank you." If the situation allows follow up, say, "This is the

---

[53] *Barnes Notes,* Albert Barnes (1798-1870)
[54] 1 Peter 1:15
[55] Matthew 7:16, 20
[56] Believers are called to holiness
[57] Ephesians 4:1-3

Lord's doing; it is not my natural disposition." Hopefully that will lead to sharing more of how one becomes kinder, more loving, more joyful… That's the fruit of the Spirit. That's a sanctified Christian.

> Jesus prayed to the Father
> For His disciples,
> "Make them holy by your truth;
> teach them your word, which is truth."[67]

May it be so!

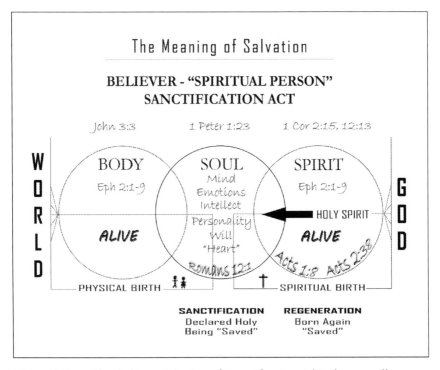

Figure 3. Sanctified believer: The Act of Sanctification. This diagram illustrates the "act of sanctification" spoken of by the Apostle Paul in Romans 12:1. It is entire submission to the will of God and the act of inviting the Holy Spirit into the mind.

---

[58] John 17:17 NLT

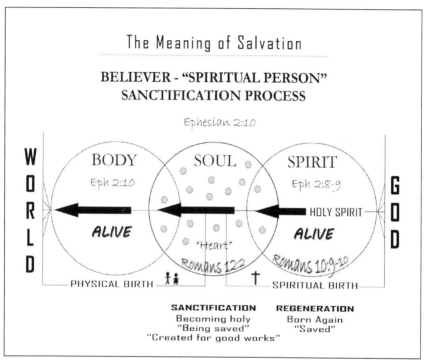

Figure 4. Sanctified believer: The Process of Sanctification. This diagram shows that the door to the heart is open and the Holy Spirit is given free access into the soul. This also illustrates sanctification but this time, the diagram shows the process of sanctification. Paul talks about it in Romans 12:2. The little circles in the fourth diagram represent values held by the individual— these personal values have "I" at the center—and now, surrendered to the Lord, every value (in time) is renewed by the indwelling Spirit who enables God to be at the center. You will see the word Sanctification under the center circle (the soul).

CHAPTER 7

SAVED FROM THE WRATH OF GOD!

The Diploma

I

Graduation is the day when students wear gowns and mortarboard caps, hear a sometimes long and boring speech, and march single file to the platform when their names are called. The solemn and long awaited moment has arrived. They will receive a diploma.

Course work is completed at a certain level of perfection acceptable to the institution for graduation and the achievement will be made part of one's resume. The well-earned diploma is placed in the hand of the graduate by the president of the institution while other notables are standing by. Congratulations are in order for a job well done. Pictures are taken and the family goes out to eat.

One could also finish with a higher grade point average than the minimum required for graduation and the words *cum laude* ("with praise") or *magna cum laude* ("with great praise") would be added to the diploma. The graduate would be proud to list that fact in a resume when applying for a job because that means the applicant was a little closer to perfection. But wait! There is a higher level than that. When the words indicating that highest level are affixed to one's resume, any hiring agent will believe this person could be called "a brain." The words are, *Summa cum laude*, "with highest academic honors," and that is a notable achievement!

For the born again Christian, there is a third aspect to his or her salvation. There is graduation day also. Some groups speak of death as a "promotion to glory." It is the death of the body not the soul or spirit. At physical death, the believer is "absent from the body and present with the Lord," so the Apostle Paul taught.[1]

> We are of good courage, I say, and prefer rather to be absent
> from the body and to be at home with the Lord.

Perhaps an angel will hand out the diplomas with Jesus standing by as the believer's Advocate. He will say, "Father, this is John (or Joan) who has believed in my work on his (or her) behalf. Please receive this believer into heaven." The believer will then hear the Father saying, "Welcome home, Child; you have finished the course. Enter and let's celebrate together!"[2] What beautiful words!

The resurrection of the dead will occur and then the believer receive a glorified, immortal body, a body that will be as perfect as Adam and Eve's bodies were when they were created. How will that happen when many saints have been dead for a long time and their bodies have turned to dust? If He chooses to, God can reach down, scoop up a handful of dirt, and recreate a believer's new, perfect body, just as He did for our original parents. One difference: believers have experienced the saving work of Jesus and as a result, the spirit, soul and body will be united again, perfectly and beautifully—and Christians will be eternally grateful.

Jesus said He was going to leave His disciples but He would come again when His disciples least expected it. His coming will be sudden, as a thief in the night. He said:

> "Behold, I am coming quickly, and My reward is with Me,
> to render to every man according to what he has done."[3]

One day, believers still living on the earth will be caught away (raptured). Once with the Lord, there will be an award ceremony for all the faithful. Later on, a court session will be held for the unfaithful who will hear their final sentencing. Since they have rejected Jesus, they will have no advocate to plead their case.

> For the Lord Himself will descend from heaven with a shout,
> with the voice of the archangel and with the trumpet of God,

---

[1] 2 Corinthians 5:8
[2] Matthew 25:21 NIV; literally, "enter the joy of your master/lord" as other versions have it.
[3] Revelation 22:12

and the dead in Christ will rise first. Then we who are alive and remain will be caught up[4] together with them in the clouds to meet the Lord in the air, and so we shall always be with the Lord.[5]

"Do not marvel at this; for an hour is coming, in which all who are in the tombs will hear His voice, and will come forth; those who did the good deeds to a resurrection of life, those who committed the evil deeds to a resurrection of judgment."[6]

As the Lord passes out diplomas to the faithful, He will give directions to each believer's new home that Jesus promised to prepare for His disciples before He went away.

In My Father's house are many dwelling places; if it were not so, I would have told you; for I go to prepare a place for you.[7]

Incidentally, did you know that if you have confessed sins and are a faithful believer, you are already the recipient of a crown? Psalm 103 records David's confession of sin, but see what he also says under the inspiration of the Spirit of God: "[The Lord] redeems your life from the pit, [and He] crowns you with lovingkindness and compassion."[8]

Note that it is our practice to mention these three nouns in reverse order: body, soul, and spirit, but God deals first with the spirit (regeneration), then with the soul (sanctification), and finally with the body (glorification) which is salvation's complete plan for reconciling believers to God. Salvation-glorification makes the final phase a reality. Spirit, soul, and now body (in that order) are ready for eternity!

---

[4] Verb in Greek, *harpazo*, means "to seize" and carry off or away by force; "to claim for one's self"; also, "to rapture" comes from this word
[5] 1 Thessalonians 4:16-17
[6] John 5:28-29, the speaker is Jesus
[7] John 14:2
[8] Psalm 103:4

II

Graduation is a time when awards are given out to those who have done well. In Matthew 25, we find the parable of the talents[9] where Jesus makes heart-warming remarks about those who use what God has given them. The "Master" is Jesus in this parable and the "slaves/servants" are those who have been entrusted with His work while He is away. They have been given gifts to use.[10] When the Master returns, He will say to the faithful:

> Well done, good and faithful slave. You were faithful with
> a few things, I will put you in charge of many things; enter
> into the joy of your master.[11]

And to the one who did not use the talents entrusted to him, the master said to him:

> You wicked, lazy slave, you knew that I reap where I did not
> sow and gather where I scattered no seed. Then you ought to
> have put my money in the bank, and on my arrival I would
> have received my money back with interest.[12]

God has given gifts to each Christian and, on the award ceremony day, He will award those who have used His gift(s) wisely. He will speak severely to those who have been lazy. It would be wise to check with the leadership of your church, asking them what they see as your spiritual gift(s).

> But to each one is given the manifestation of the Spirit for
> the common good.[13]

III

It is reported that the word "glory" occurs 359 times in 331 verses in one version of the Bible.

In the Old Testament, the root of the Hebrew word for "glory" is "to be heavy or weighty," and is used metaphorically to mean something grievous or

---

[9] A weight of about 96 pounds; "used metaphorically in the New Testament for mental and spiritual attainments or gifts." -International Standard Bible Encyclopedia
[10] See 1 Corinthians 12
[11] Matthew 25:23
[12] Matthew 25:26, 28
[13] 1 Corinthians 12:7, the verses that follow speak of spiritual gifts

burdensome. It is also used for the visual manifestation of God's glory. Exodus 40:34 tells us, "Then a cloud covered the tent of the congregation, and the glory of the LORD filled the tabernacle."

The Greek word in the New Testament for "glory" means "opinion," "estimate," and therefore "honorable" resulting from a good opinion. It is, according to the Greek lexicon,[14] "the nature and acts of God in self-manifestation, i.e., what He essentially is and does," It is also used of "the state into which believers enter after this life having been transformed into the likeness of Christ." That state of blessedness is salvation-glorification. What else does the Bible say about sanctification-glorification? That leads us to three questions:

Who will be glorified?

What is a glorified body?

When will our bodies be glorified?

Who Will Be Glorified?

The Bible states that those who are "conformed to the image of His Son" Jesus Christ as Redeemer and Risen Lord will be glorified. Examine the following verses:

> Romans 8 verses 29-30
> For those whom He [God] foreknew, He also predestined to become conformed to the image of His Son, so that He [the Son] would be the firstborn among many brethren; and these whom He predestined, He also called; and these whom He called, He also justified; and these whom He justified, He also glorified.

> Philippians 3:20-21
> But our citizenship is in heaven. And we eagerly await a Savior from there, the Lord Jesus Christ, who, by the power that enables him to bring everything under his control, will transform our lowly bodies so that they will be like his glorious body.

---

[14] "A dictionary, especially one of an ancient language such as Greek or Hebrew," —Free Dictionary

This third aspect of salvation, glorification, is the believer's crowning glory—literally! The Apostle Paul says we will have a spiritual body at our physical death, and at the resurrection of the dead (bodies), we will have a new physical body. God will create a new body for every believer and join together once again the body, soul and spirit in a union that is truly perfect and beyond temptation. Believers' bodies will be changed so "they will be like His glorious body." This is glorification! It is then that God will deal the final blow to Satan, condemning him and Hell with its entire inhabitants to the Lake of Fire for eternity.

What Is A Glorified Body?

To understand what new glorious bodies will be like, a few comments about Adam will help, and the Scripture's descriptions of Christ's glorious body will help even more.

Will the creation of the new body be like God's creation of Adam whom he formed "of the dust of the ground?" I think so. Artists picture the day of the resurrection of the dead as people coming up out of their graves, but I submit there isn't any trace of people buried at sea or of Old Testament saints on land. Sharks and other fish no doubt made short work of the former and strong winds may have blown the dust of the latter, here, there, and everywhere!

So where are their remains? There's plenty of dust on the globe and little evidence of those early saints. But it doesn't matter! It will be a new body, perfect in every way. Our Creator will reach down, take some dust, and form a new body for every believer who ever lived and that will be a greater miracle than reaching down, taking some dust, and forming the one man of Genesis 2. Of Adam it is written, "[God] breathed into his nostrils the breath of life; and man became a living soul." God will reunite our spirit and soul—already a new creation through regeneration and sanctification—with the newly created physical body.

God is pleased to transform us in our entirety and make every believer a perfect finished product, having a glorified body, glorified soul, and glorified spirit!

Keep in mind that the body is a believer's temporary dwelling—remember, the Apostle Paul called the body a tent. It is something that in time wears out. Enemies who make martyrs of believers only bring martyrs a fantastic blessing. Their physical lives are cut short and their bodies begin the process of turning to dust, but the real person who lived in those temporary dwellings which have been "torn down," are promoted to Glory—and that's a synonym for Heaven! They immediately experience glorification of soul and spirit and will soon be the recipient of the glorification of their bodies on the day of the resurrection of the dead.

Don't ever be afraid of death. The real person within is then released to enjoy that next and final aspect of salvation. I daresay an angel will be present to take each believer's hand,[15] or more amazing, maybe the Lord Jesus Himself[16] will lead the believer to the Father in Heaven, forever changed and forever blessed!

Now we can examine the Scriptures to see what they tell us about the glorified body. First, remember Philippians 3:20-21 that is quoted above and especially the last phrase: "Jesus Christ… will transform our lowly bodies so that they will be like his glorious body."

How can we describe His glorious body after His resurrection? What hints can we glean as we review Scriptures that offer us clues about His glorified body? They will help understand what the glorified body of each believer will be like.

Here's a snapshot.

Following His resurrection, Jesus was not a ghost. He could speak and be heard. He could be seen and be touched. He prepared a fire, cooked a breakfast, and ate.

There are a number of additional texts that can be examined. For example, Mary Magdalene, according to John 20, went to the tomb on the first day of the week and found it empty. In distress, she spoke to a man standing nearby whom she thought was the gardener. She did not recognize him even by his question directed to her. Then He gently spoke her name and she instantly knew Him.

> Jesus said to her, "Woman, why are you weeping? Whom are
> you seeking?" Supposing Him to be the gardener, she said to
> Him, "Sir, if you have carried Him away, tell me where you
> have laid Him, and I will take Him away." Jesus said to her,

---

[15] Hebrews 1:14 (NIV), "Are not all angels ministering spirits sent to serve those who will inherit salvation?"

[16] John 14:3, "If I go and prepare a place for you, I will come again and receive you to Myself, that where I am, there you may be also."

"Mary!" She turned and said to Him in Hebrew, "Rabboni!" (which means, Teacher).[17]

Another example involves two disciples who left Jerusalem after the Lord's death. They too had an encounter with the resurrected Jesus as they were heading for the little village of Emmaus. The Gospel of Luke tells us in Chapter 24 that although Jesus joined them along the way, verse 16 says, "… they were prevented [or, kept] from recognizing him." The Gospel of Mark says He appeared to them "in another form" but Mark doesn't elaborate further on that comment.[18]

In the Luke 24 text, His companions referred to Him as a Stranger. The original word suggests "dwelling in a neighborhood as a stranger." The text goes on to say:

> One of them, named Cleopas, answered and said to Him, "Are You the only one visiting Jerusalem and unaware of the things which have happened here in these days?"[19]

Another translation says it well: "You must be the only person in Jerusalem who hasn't heard about all the things that have happened there the last few days."[20]

The two disciples told this stranger their disappointment concerning their hopes they had placed in Jesus of Nazareth. These hopes were dashed by His tragic death, they explained. The account goes on to say they went into a house to eat.

> When He had reclined [at the table to eat] with them, He took the bread and blessed it, and breaking it, He began giving it to them. Then their eyes were opened and they recognized Him; and He vanished from their sight.[21]

Eight days later, Jesus suddenly appeared in their midst of the gathered disciples. Again note that He appeared in their midst twice and did not come through the doors either time. Suddenly, He was there!

---

[17] John 20:15-16
[18] Mark 16:12
[19] Luke 24:18
[20] Luke 24:18 NLT
[21] Luke 24:30-31

> So when it was evening on that day, the first day of the week, and when the doors were shut where the disciples were for fear of the Jews, Jesus came and stood in their midst and said to them, "Peace be with you." When He said this, He showed them His hands and His side. The disciples then rejoiced when they saw the Lord and heard Him speak.[22]

The first time Jesus showed Himself to His disciples, Thomas was not there. When they told him the good news, he said he would not believe them until he saw the prints of the nails. The second time he was present and the Lord spoke to him directly about His "wounds." Presumably, the wounds were healed but there were visible scars.

> Jesus said to him, "Reach here with your finger, and see My hands; and reach here with your hand and put it into My side; and do not be unbelieving, but believing."[23]

When believers get to Heaven, will they see those scars as well? I rather think they will...lest we forget the horrendous price in human suffering that was paid.

In John 21, there is the account of the meeting in Galilee. The place was the Lake of Galilee (also called the Sea of Tiberius). Jesus was standing on the shore looking at the disciples who were trying to catch fish a hundred yards or so off shore. They could see Him but did not recognize Him. All night, they had been out in the boat fishing but without success. Jesus called to them and told them to throw their net in the water on the right side of the boat. They did and it was so full of fish—153 large fish, was the count—they were barely able to pull the net to shore. They succeeded but to their utter amazement, the net was not torn.

While still in the boat, John, the writer of the fourth Gospel, recognized the miracle for what it was and identified the Man on the shore who spoke. He exclaimed, "It is the Lord!" And it was. According to John 21:9, when they went ashore they "saw a charcoal fire already laid and fish placed on it, and bread." Jesus then invited them to bring some of their fish to cook so there would be enough for all to have breakfast together. Amazing! Charcoal wasn't just lying around on the sandy shore, neither was a lit fire!

---

[22] John 20:19-20
[23] John 20:27

Back in Jerusalem, He appeared to them, frightening them because of His sudden appearance in the room. Then, reassuring them that He was not a ghost, He asked for something to eat.

> They gave Him a piece of a broiled fish; and He took it and ate it before them.[24]

What do the Scriptures tell us about the Lord's glorified body? Here are several observations: [25]

> ➤ He had a human body in shape and form with flesh and bones.
> ➤ He could withhold His personal identification or reveal it.
> ➤ He was recognizable when He spoke a person's name and when He offered prayer.
> ➤ He could appear and vanish at will.
> ➤ His recent wounds were visible and could be touched perhaps implying they were healed. (Another explanation: the actual holes were still visible, but there was no blood. Thomas is invited to put his finger into the Lord's hands and side.)
> ➤ He could defy material hindrances such as locks, doors and walls.
> ➤ He did manual labor.
> ➤ He ate.
> ➤ His ascension (that soon occurred) defied gravity.

When Will Our Bodies Be Glorified?

Please remember a point made in Chapter 3, that the Bible is more concerned about events than time. Those who try to pin point the dates of Christ's Second Coming, the resurrection of the dead, or The Tribulation are just as mistaken as those who tried to pin point the exact day and year that Jesus was to be born. In 1 Corinthians 15:42, 52 and 53, Paul highlights events, making no note of time. It's the "what" not the "when":

> So also is the resurrection of the dead. It is sown a perishable body, it is raised an imperishable body… For the trumpet will sound, the dead will be raised imperishable, and we will be changed. For the perishable must clothe itself with the imperishable, and the mortal with immortality.

---

[24] Luke 24:42-43
[25] Mark 16, Luke 24, John 20, and Acts 1

There is confusion even among Christians about the burial of a body in a grave and the resurrection of the body. At the moment of physical death, the real person that lives inside the body, which is the soul and spirit, goes to be with Lord. The body is a temporary dwelling place for the soul and spirit, as noted above. The body is destined to return to the ground, "dust to dust."[26] The resurrection of the dead involves the body not the soul and spirit.

Writing to the Thessalonians, Paul tells them that those who have already died will return with Jesus at His second coming: Here's the event:

> For if we believe that Jesus died and rose again, even so God will bring with Him those who have fallen asleep [died] in Jesus. [27]

Consider these points: The spiritual or immaterial part of Christ's glorified body was prominent and His physical or material part, His flesh and bones, were subject to it. The reverse is true of our present state on earth; our spiritual self is subject to the material or physical body. Living on Planet Earth, walls and locks keep the human body out. But they did not keep out Jesus living in a glorified body!

Additionally, God created Adam with a perfect body, soul and spirit. Some may raise the question, if Adam was perfect, how could he have sinned? Here is the answer: God gave Adam a will to decide whether to yield to the devil's challenge or reject it. God knew this was sure to come. Adam yielded and in doing so, disobeyed the Lord.

Why would the Lord grant Adam and Eve that privilege? Wasn't that a dangerous privilege, even a foolish thing to do? Yes, that was a dangerous thing to do, but no, what God does is never a foolish thing. Why did He do it then? Love is the reason. Love is a matter of choice, for without choice, man would have been a robot.

At the time of the resurrection of our bodies, we will no longer be subject to the physical laws of the universe. The reverse will be true: those laws will be subject to us as God puts us to work in our glorified bodies. Work? Did I say "work"? Yes, I did.

Do you object to the statement that Christians will be working in glorified bodies? Jesus worked in His glorified body, lighting a fire and fixing breakfast for His disciples on the shore of Lake Tiberius.

---

[26] See Genesis 3:19 and Ecclesiastes 3:20
[27] 1 Thessalonians 4:14-17

God will have a lot of exciting God-honoring things for us to do in Heaven. Have you read the account of Adam and Eve while they were in the Garden of Eden? They were not in the Garden to laze around; God had assigned Adam jobs to do. He told them:

> Be fruitful and multiply, and fill the earth, and subdue it;
> and rule over the fish of the sea and over the birds of the sky
> and over every living thing that moves on the earth.[28]

Bible's view of the body: The body is made from dust and God promises it will return to dust.[29] The body is a tent, a temporary dwelling place that wears out. "While we are at home in the body, we are absent from the Lord" but at death, believers are "absent from the body and at home with the Lord."[30]

At interment or burial, the tent wherein the person lived while on earth is buried but a Christian loved one is not six-feet-under. No, he or she is not there at all, but with the Lord, no longer needing the worn out tent.

The Christian will have a new glorified body. The coming changes for the believer are exciting, miraculous, and permanent!

> Blessed and holy is the one who has a part in the first resurrection; over these the second death has no power, but they will be priests of God and of Christ and will reign with Him for a thousand years.[31]

SUMMARY STATEMENT
We have everlasting life and are saved from **SIN**
— this is regeneration.
We have a holy life and are being saved from **SELF**
— this is sanctification.
We will have a new perfect body and be saved from
THE WRATH OF GOD
AND THE SECOND DEATH
— this is glorification.
Hallelujah!

---

[28] Genesis 1:28
[29] Genesis 3:19
[30] 2 Corinthians 5:6-8
[31] Revelation 20:6

God, working to demonstrate His love for us, gave us His only Son Jesus, the God-Man, who spent thirty years in Podunk and three years teaching culture-shattering messages. He was sent from Heaven to do His Heavenly Father's will and He did it. His disciples were puzzled about the "from Heaven" part until they saw the risen Christ in His glorified body.

Alas, the religious leaders of His day had deaf ears and hard hearts and they choose to reject His words because He was a round peg who didn't fit into their square holes. He was unable to get through to them. But their stubbornness and pride that resulted in railroading Jesus to the cross fit exactly into the Father's perfect plan. The Messiah's death made it possible for the curse of sin to be overcome. Yes, in Adam all die but in Christ, all are made alive![32]

In his article "What Is Glorification?" Matt Slick explained that since Christ was the first resurrected from the dead in a glorified body, He represents the first fruits of resurrection and the resurrection of believers will follow. Slick concluded that "His resurrection is the promise and guarantee of our future resurrection." [33]

> You are invited to let the Holy Spirit give you new life.
> This is regeneration!
> This is to be born again.
> This is to live for Jesus!
> Let the Holy Spirit guide your life
> into all truth and reveal to you
> God's direction for your life.
> This is sanctification!
> This is to become holy,
> one victory at a time!
> Live forever! You will have a brand
> new body, never again to experience
> aches and pains, weeping, or death.
> This is glorification!
> Magnificent crowns will be awarded.

[32] 1 Corinthians 15:22
[33] Christian Apologetics & Research Ministry website

This is the time Jesus will be crowned King of kings and Lord of Lords. Believers will live forever under the watchful eye of the glorified Christ. He will reign over His Father's creation and there will be perfect peace for a thousand years, [34] peace that has eluded all mankind since the day of Adam's fateful fall into sin. [35]

"He who testifies to these things says, 'Yes, I am coming quickly.'"[36] When the Father says it is time, suddenly, the Lord Jesus Christ will be here![37] The Second Advent will be a reality.

"Amen. Come, Lord Jesus."[38]

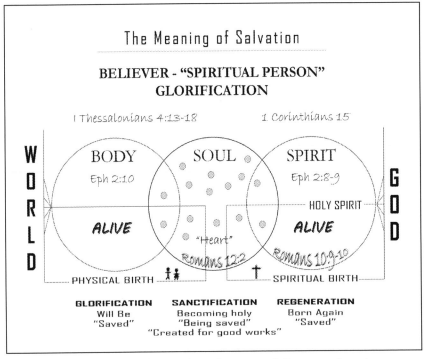

Figure 5. Glorified believer. This diagram, following the chapter on glorification, illustrates the renewal of the body at the resurrection. At this point, spirit, soul, and body are all renewed and salvation is complete. The word "Glorification" appears under the left circle labeled the "body."

---

[34] See the imprisonment of Satan for 1000 years, Revelation 20:1

[35] Genesis 2

[36] Revelation 22:20

[37] See Acts 1:7

[38] Revelation 22:20

CHAPTER 8

FIRST STEP OF OBEDIENCE

Water Baptism

I

Imagine a small group of believers gathered one beautiful summer day alongside a crystal clear stream in the beautiful Adirondack Mountains. I, a brand new pastor, was ready to conduct my first baptismal service in such a setting. I stepped into the stream and hoped my face didn't reveal my ignorance of mountain streams nor betray what my body was feeling: "This is very, very cold!"

After baptizing two believers, an older, single woman stepped into the water. Standing in the middle of the stream, she professed her faith in Christ. Then as I placed my hands on her to proceed with the baptism, she said quietly but very firmly, "Don't touch me!" Now that was going to be a difficult job baptizing without touching since my method of baptizing was immersion. Puzzled, I watched as she slowly slid down into the water once, twice, and then three times. I wondered if this was some new procedure in rural New York State. Finishing, she turned and said, "I'm ready now." She knew about cold mountain streams and that's how she handled it. Believers watching knew the very cold water was part of this wonderful moment and they warmed the air with singing praises to God.

There is much confusion concerning the mode of baptism and the words to use when baptizing candidates. There is also confusion concerning the meaning of baptism. Catholics believe that the rite or ritual conveys grace. Some evangelical churches believe it to be a prerequisite for church membership while others see it as symbolic of the death and resurrection of Jesus Christ and unrelated to membership. Some denominations insist on re-baptizing when a believer moves into their churches from another denomination and requests membership. Others require the believer to be immersed three times, viewing once as inadequate. Still others believe one must be baptized in Jesus' Name only. There are some Christian groups that do not believe baptism is necessary for our present age.

Sadly, some make their mode of baptism a basis for fellowship.

There are churches where parents present their babies, agreeing to raise them in the Christian faith, and the babies are baptized by sprinkling a little water on their heads. There are other churches where babies are presented to God in an act of dedication, just as Hannah presented her son Samuel to the Lord[1]. No water is used in this act called dedication. Baptism is reserved for those children who later make a personal confession of faith in Christ as Lord and Savior; this is called "believer's baptism."

There are at least three methods of baptizing: aspersion (sprinkling), affusion (pouring), and immersion. A little boy raced up the slope from the Lake Erie shore yelling to a young friend, "Hey, c'm on down; they're dunkin' people!" A baptismal service was in progress at a summer camp meeting and candidates were waiting their turn while others on the shore served as witnesses. The baptismal method was immersion (dipping a new believer into the water completely) rather than sprinkling or pouring water on the head. The boy's comment meant he saw people being baptized by immersion.

In this study, we dig deeper into the Word of God and examine the biblical concept of baptism. I will suggest why baptism is necessary and why one method is preferable. What does the Bible say? Here are some of the major issues to investigate:

1. Why be baptized?
    * Jesus' experience
    * Jesus' command
    * Peter's practice
    * Paul's practice
2. What does the term "baptism" mean?
    * Greek terms: *bapto, baptizo*
    * Symbol and picture
3. Questions concerning baptism that have been debated by godly theologians over the centuries.

---

[1] 1 Samuel 1:27-28

104

4. What is important is this: Don't let semantics confuse you and deter you from identifying with Jesus as your Savior and Lord in whatever way you are persuaded after you have studied this chapter.

    - Can one be baptized more than once?
    - Is it a prerequisite for church membership?
    - Should infants or adults be baptized?
    - How much water is appropriate: sprinkling, pouring, or immersion?
    - Is a three-fold baptism required?
    - Is the formula a "Jesus-only" formula?
    - Is baptism required as a part of the regeneration (born again) process?

II

Why Be Baptized?

The experience of Jesus. According to Mark 1, Jesus approached John the Baptist and requested John baptize Him. This was water baptism which Mark calls "a baptism of repentance for the remission of sins." Repentance was John's message. Paul refers to John's baptism similarly in Acts 19:3 and the phrase used there, "baptized into John," tells us baptism was to show publicly one's submission to John's teaching. By submitting to John's baptism, Jesus affirmed John's ministry and publicly demonstrated that He was identifying with God's ongoing work.

When John baptized Jesus, the Holy Spirit came down upon Jesus in the form of a dove. This latter event is referred to as "the baptism of the Spirit" which was repeated (without the external sign of the dove) at Pentecost when the Holy Spirit came down upon the church at its birth.[2]

The disciples of Jesus were also baptized in water before Pentecost as John 3:22 suggests. Jesus Himself baptized the first of His disciples and then most likely committed the work of baptism to them for subsequent believers (John 4:2). They were baptized with (or, in) water, but not filled with the Holy Spirit at that point.

The command of Jesus. This is commonly called "The Great Commission." Jesus uttered this command to His disciples after His resurrection. This became their marching orders. Jesus spoke to them, saying:

---

[2] Acts 2; 1 Cor. 12:13

> All authority has been given to Me in heaven and
> on earth. Go therefore and make disciples of all the
> nations, baptizing them in the name of the Father
> and the Son and the Holy Spirit, teaching them
> to observe all that I commanded you; and lo, I am
> with you always, even to the end of the age.[108]

The disciples did not baptize new believers with the Holy Spirit; God did that; they baptized with (or, in) water. And this is what they were supposed to do according to Matthew 28. Jesus explained to them that making disciples meant they were to baptize all nations and teach them, that is, "impart instruction, instill doctrine, explain or expound things" (Greek Lexicon).

Baptism was not an option of the newly evangelized; it was a command. Christ did not say, "If you want to be baptized…," as is often the incorrect opening phrase of a church bulletin announcement for a baptismal service. To *not* want to be baptized in the early church would have seriously brought into question the genuineness of conversion. In those days, religion was integrated into one's daily life—as it should be with contemporary Christians. Baptism was one way to let others know they were no longer part of their former way of life.

Peter's practice. Following the momentous events on the Day of Pentecost, three thousand people received Peter's words and were baptized.[4] The next verse tells us that an intensive teaching program followed. This baptism refers to water baptism. Compare the following (See gray box).

> While Peter was speaking in the home of the Roman centurion,
> the Holy Spirit came upon the assembled household. This surprised
> Peter because he was talking to Gentiles. He said, "Surely no
> one can stand in the way of their being baptized with water.
> They have received the Holy Spirit just as we have.[110]

Paul's practice. In Acts 19, we have the account of Paul's first contact with the Ephesians. He found twelve disciples there and asked them if they

---

[3] Matthew 28:18-20
[4] Acts 2:42
[5] Acts 10:47 NIV

had received the Holy Spirit when they believed. Paul finds they had only heard John the Baptist preach and had submitted to his baptism. It is assumed that Apollos, who knew only of John's baptism until he was instructed further by Priscilla and Aquila, baptized them "into John."[6] They were John's disciples and had not heard that the Holy Spirit had come. Apparently they were faithful in waiting to hear that their Messiah was Jesus of Nazareth, affirmed by His resurrection from the dead and by the coming of the Holy Spirit. Paul shares the Good News with the Ephesians, and then baptizes them "in the Name of the Lord Jesus." Following this, Paul laid his hands on them and "the Holy Spirit came upon them."

The preaching map laid out for the apostles in Acts 1:8, "Jerusalem, Samaria, Judea, and the uttermost part of the earth," was now complete, not that all people heard, but that the points of contact were reached. In the kindness of God, each group[7] heard the Gospel, and each one believed in Jesus' death as the atonement for their sins. Then both Peter (in Samaria and Caesarea) and Paul (in Asia Minor, Macedonia and Greece) baptized them with water and were amazed that Samaritans and Gentiles were also filled with the Spirit. This was an act of a gracious God to minimize the discrimination that already existed among these groups.

Paul tells the Corinthian Christians he didn't baptize anyone in his name.[8] He explains that when he was in Ephesus, he only baptized two men and the household of Stephanas.[9] Others would have been baptized by Paul's associates or by those appointed as elders of the developing churches.

Jesus, Peter and Paul do not give details concerning the mode of baptism since the Jews already practiced it; they baptized new converts to Judaism. To be baptized as a Christian was a very serious step in the early centuries of the Church; and it still is today for converted Muslims or Jews. The Mosaic Law as amended by the rabbis over the years required the use of water in ritual cleansing (see Leviticus 11:25, 11:40; and 15:5-7). Adam Clarke's Comment on Baptism:

> [Baptism] was the criterion of a Jew's conversion; and when a Jew had received baptism in this name [the Name of Jesus], he was excluded from all communication with his countrymen;

---

[6] Acts 18-19:1, also see ISBE: Apollos, and Ray Stedman: Halfway Christian
[7] Acts 2, 8, 10, 19
[8] 1 Corinthians 1:13-15
[9] 1 Corinthians 1:14-16

and no man would have forfeited such privileges but on the fullest and clearest conviction. This baptism was a very powerful means to prevent their apostasy; they had, by receiving baptism in the name of Jesus, renounced Judaism and all the political advantages connected with it; and they found it indispensably necessary to make the best use of that holy religion which they had received in its stead.

...These 3000 persons left the scribes and Pharisees, and put themselves under the teaching of the apostles, professing the Christian doctrine, and acknowledging that Christ was come, and that he who was lately crucified by the Jews was the promised and only Messiah; and in this faith they were baptized.[10]

In Acts 10, we see Peter's emphasis on water baptism, but the unusual fact here is that the filling or baptism of the Holy Spirit came first and the water baptism second. In Acts 19:5-6, we find the reverse order. Apparently, the order is not important. What is important is that they were willing to testify publicly to their faith by submitting to baptism.

III

Definition of the word "baptize"

How is the Greek word verb *baptizo* defined in the Greek dictionary? The definition is as follows:

1. to dip repeatedly, to immerse, to submerge (of vessels sunk)
2. to cleanse by dipping or submerging, to wash, to make clean with water, to wash one's self, bathe
3. to overwhelm

There is a second similar Greek word, *bapto*, which is not to be confused with *baptizo* according to the late James Montgomery Boice, who wrote in Bible Study Magazine:

---

[10] Clarke, A. (1837). *The Holy Bible: a Commentary and Critical Notes (Act 2)*. Volume 5. New York: T. Mason & G. Lane.

The clearest example that shows the meaning of *baptizo* is a text from the Greek poet and physician Nicander, who lived about 200 B.C. It is a recipe for making pickles and is helpful because it uses both words. Nicander says that in order to make a pickle, the vegetable should first be "dipped" (*bapto*) into boiling water and then "baptized" (*baptizo*) in the vinegar solution. Both verbs concern the immersing of vegetables in a solution. But the first is temporary. The second, the act of baptizing the vegetable, produces a permanent change.[11]

The lexicon calls John's baptism "[a] purification rite by which men on confessing their sins were bound to spiritual reformation, obtained the pardon of their past sins and became qualified for the benefits of the Messiah's kingdom soon to be set up. It was a public act of an inward change of heart. It was "repentance," (which literally means "to change the mind")."

In the Old Testament, Paul says of the Israelites, "all were baptized into Moses in the cloud and in the sea."[12] This is an unusual use of the word "baptize" but Paul sees the similarity of identification.

Baptism is a public demonstration of an inward decision of the will to break with one's former worldview and submit to a new body of teaching—in this case, to Christ as Savior and Lord and to the Christian faith. Jews baptized proselytes and declared them to be, following the baptism, a "new creation" or "a new person." Actually, they took this concept to an absurd degree reasoning that if a proselyte was baptized, he was a totally new person and his former family no longer existed. Therefore, he could actually one day be married to his own mother if she were also converted to Judaism, baptized and made a "new person." They would not be guilty of incest.[13]

Catholics call baptism and the Eucharist *sacraments* (two of several) and believe that by participating in these sacred rites, they literally receive grace. Eucharist means "Thanksgiving" which most Protestants call communion or The Lord's Table. Webster's dictionary defines a sacrament as a rite or observance "ordained by Christ and held to be a means of divine grace or to be a sign or symbol of a spiritual reality." In the fourth century, Augustine defined sacraments as "outward and visible signs of an inward and spiritual

---

[11] Boice, J. M., (May, 1989). *Bible Study Magazine*.
[12] 1 Corinthians 10:2
[13] Kaufmann, Kohler, Krauss, S. Baptism. Retrieved from http://jewishencyclopedia.com/articles/2456-baptism

grace." Catholics believe it is a means of grace while the Protestants generally hold that it is a sign or symbol of a spiritual reality.

Most Protestant groups observe both baptism and communion but may call them practices or ordinances. This latter word is defined as "something ordained by deity; a prescribed usage, practice or ceremony." The Salvation Army did not used to call itself a church, but some of their groups now use this term and have regular worship services although they neither baptize nor serve communion.

IV

Water baptism as a symbol and a picture

According to Webster's dictionary, a symbol is "something that stands for or suggests something else by reason of relationship, association, convention, or accidental resemblance, especially, a visible sign of something invisible." In his commentary *Word Pictures,* Robertson explained, "It should be said also that a symbol is not the reality, but the picture of the reality".[14] The Apostle Paul refers to this in Romans 6 where he says that to be baptized in water is a symbol of our death to sin, and coming from the water, a symbol of our resurrection, that is, a coming into a new life.

In baptism, believers re-enact symbolically Christ's death and resurrection, and, more than that, show that they believe those events occurred on their behalf. Of course, this act is credible but only if one has confessed one's sins and declared Jesus Christ as Lord.

Referring to the words of F.B. Meyer, Robertson said "The picture in baptism points two ways, backwards to Christ's death and burial and to our death to sin, [and it points] forward to Christ's resurrection from the dead and to our new life pledged by the coming out of the watery grave to walk on the other side of the baptismal grave." [15]

---

[14] Robertson, A.T. *Robertson's Word pictures of the New Testament.* Retrieved from http://www.biblestudytools.com/commentaries/robertsons-word-pictures
[15] Robertson, A.T. Commentary on Romans 6:4. *Robertson's Word Pictures of the New Testament.* Retrieved from https://www.studylight.org/commentary/romans/6-4. html.

V

Questions concerning baptism

1. How often?

The Jews observed Passover once every year. Jesus established what is commonly called, the Last Supper, at the conclusion of the Passover meal. In place of the Passover, the early church substituted a meal they called the Agapé Meal (Love Feast, or what some call a Fellowship Meal) and then concluded the meal with the communion service. Paul tells the Corinthians, "As often as you partake…" (1 Cor. 11), leaving the frequency of time to the local church.

As to baptism, once was deemed sufficient since it placed the baptized believer clearly in the Christian camp. It was an act that need not be repeated. It was repeated in the case of the Ephesian disciples (Acts 19) who were baptized twice—and had they been proselytes to the Jewish religion originally, they were baptized three times. Reasons are given below under the discussion of infant baptism.

2. Church membership?

Does water baptism make one a member of a particular local church? The Catholics would say yes: once baptized a Catholic, they say, always a Catholic. Some Protestant churches do not regard the baptism of other churches to be valid and require believers to be re-baptized for membership. The danger of tying water baptism to church membership is that it confuses faith and works. Baptism is the public expression of one's inward faith. Church membership is a "good work" that a believer does. Many evangelical churches see the responsibilities of membership as different from requirements for baptism and keep the two practices separate to avoid confusion.

3. Infants or adults?

The early Christians were adults who, by baptism, showed that their allegiance was to the Lord Jesus Christ, not Caesar. There is an implication that children may have also been baptized (Acts 16:35) but that is by no means certain. The question about children brought up in a Christian home is more difficult. Funk and Wagnall's Encyclopedia propose, "Infants were probably baptized in the early church, following the Jewish understanding that even the youngest children belong to the covenant community." Another view is that since children are presented in dedication to the Lord they are under the umbrella of protection of their Christian parents, and are therefore part of the new covenant.

Some argue that children should be baptized on the basis of several passages in the book of Acts where Luke mentions a certain person was baptized "and his/her household." Robertson, quoting Forneaux, comments on the Lydia passage:

> This statement cannot be claimed as any argument for infant baptism, since the Greek word [household] may mean her servants or her work-people (Furneaux) In the household baptisms (Cornelius, Lydia, the jailor, Crispus) one sees "infants" or not according to his predilections or preferences.[16]

Since baptism involves symbols, it is reasonable to suppose that children should not be baptized before they are old enough to understand abstract concepts, "this stands for that." For baptism to be meaningful, the child must understand that the water stands for death and coming up from the water stands for resurrection. They must also be able to understand both the notion of personal sin and the concept of consequences: "All have sinned and come short of the glory of God...The wages of sin is death."[17] They must understand (and this may be the easier part) that Another—that is, Christ—took the punishment for their wrongdoing (sins) by dying in their place.

Elders should question children well before admitting a child to baptism and they should also receive positive testimony from the parent(s) that the child is sensitive to the commands and correction of the Lord.

4. How much water?

Sprinkling is a little, pouring is more, and immersion is a lot. There have been arguments over John's baptism. Did people stand in the water while he poured water over their heads? Or did he immerse them? We do not know. Since the word baptized is used in connection with the Israelites, how much water did Moses use? Actually, none. The waters piled up either side of the Israelites, but they came through on dry land![18] There was a lot of water but it didn't touch them. The theological idea comes to the fore here: it was an

---

[16] Robertson, A.T. Commentary on Acts 16:15. *Robertson's Word Pictures of the New Testament.* Retrieved from https://www.studylight.org/commentary/romans/6-4.html.

[17] Romans 3:23 and 6:23

[18] 1 Cor. 10 and Exodus 14:16, 24, 29

irrevocable commitment to a new life under Moses, and a clear break with the life of the past. What is recorded is that "the waters were like a wall to them on their right hand and on their left." [19] If the waters piled up on either side of them, we may assume they walked under the waters." They marched over on dry ground; not a drop of water touched them! When the waters closed up, Pharaoh's men were swallowed; not one escaped. As for the Israelites, there was no turning back.

Decades of arguments over the appropriate quantity of water for baptism have been fruitless and a waste of time.

Why then insist on immersion? Because it is a wonderful picture of the death and resurrection of Jesus Christ! It is He who Christians have declared as their Savior and Lord. Romans six certainly suggest that this is a symbol of the New Covenant.

> Therefore we have been buried with
> Him through baptism into death,
> so that as Christ was raised from the
> dead through the glory of the Father,
> so we too might walk in newness of life. [125]

Sprinkling is a great biblical symbol as well, but it is an Old Testament symbol of purification or cleansing. Not inappropriate, but not as powerful either since the New Covenant eclipses the Old.

5. Three-fold immersion?

There are certain Christian communities of godly people who are convinced one should be immersed once in the name of the Father, once in the name of the Son, and once in the name of the Holy Spirit. Presumably, they base this on the Matthew 28:19 passage that reads: "Go therefore and make disciples of all the nations, baptizing them in the name of the Father and the Son and the Holy Spirit." The clue that such a practice is not necessary is found in the word "name" which is singular and not plural. The Hebrew concept is that "name" stands for who the person is or what the person will do

---

[19] Exodus 14:29b
[20] Romans 6:4

or be in life. Father, Son and Holy Spirit are not names per se, but expressions of the "Name" which is more properly "Yahweh" or the "I Am."

Father, Son, and Holy Spirit are three roles our God plays to effect our salvation. As to the characteristics of God, or Yahweh, what is true of the Father is true of the Son and what is true of the Father and Son is true of the Holy Spirit. Unfortunately, some groups hold that unless believers submit to a three-fold baptism, their baptisms are not valid. To baptize with one dip into the water in the Name of the Father and of the Son and of the Holy Spirit is to cover all the bases.

6. Baptized in the Name of Jesus only?

There are a few groups of godly Christians who believe that the formula should include only the Name of Jesus since Acts speaks of new converts being baptized in the Name of Jesus. Paige (quoted in Robertson's Word Pictures) says, "Luke does not give the form of words used in baptism by the Apostles, but merely states the fact that they baptized those who acknowledged Jesus as Messiah or as Lord."[21] Unfortunately some of these groups hold that being baptized in the Name of the Father, the Son, and the Holy Spirit is invalid, and one must be re-baptized according to their formula. That is unfortunate because it closes the door to fellowship with those not of their persuasion.

As noted above, there is no difference in the "Name" of the Father, Son or Holy Spirit when understood in the Hebrew and Greek sense. It is not "in the Name of the Father and in the Name of the Son and in the Name of the Holy Spirit." Names describe character in the Bible and the character of the Father, Son, and Holy Spirit is one. I don't see a problem with using as a formula, "I baptize you in the Name of Jesus." That shows one has submitted to the teachings of Jesus Christ. Others, using the traditional formula, show a submission to the Triune God. One cannot fault the one or the other nor should anyone make their position the basis for fellowship. That would violate the law of love.

7. What about baptismal regeneration?

Those who believe in this doctrine base it on Acts 2:38, "Peter said to them, 'Repent, and each of you be baptized in the name of Jesus Christ for the forgiveness of your sins; and you will receive the gift of the Holy Spirit.'" For this group, one's salvation is not complete until one submits to water

---

[21] Robertson, A. T. (2015). *Word Pictures in the New Testament: Acts.* Aeterna Press

baptism. The important day of one's conversion is not the day that one "goes to the altar" or stands publicly to profess faith in Christ but the day of one's baptism. These church groups generally keep water in their baptismal tank all the time so they can baptize a new believer quickly, just like the episode involving the Ethiopian Eunuch who, believing and requesting baptism, was duly baptized by Philip[22].

Are these folks heretics? No. But there is danger in these practices. If they actually believe something must be added to the redemptive work of Christ that would be crossing the line.

Alas, too many evangelicals believe they can be baptized when they get around to it. They don't think much of their experience in Christ when they decide they don't want to announce it publicly! Water baptism is important but it is not part of the package that brings about new life in Christ. Paul wrote this to the Ephesians clarifying the issue:

> In him we have redemption through his blood, the forgiveness of sins, in accordance with the riches of God's grace.[23]

> For it is by grace you have been saved, through faith--and this not from yourselves, it is the gift of God--not by works, so that no-one can boast.[24]

Baptismal regeneration is not supported by other biblical references.

VI

Calling people to an altar for conversion within a church building or having them stand in a public service to acknowledge they are trusting in Christ as Savior and Lord are great occasions. But these practices should not replace the baptism that the Lord Himself commanded. Baptism allows a new convert to make a statement to the unsaved as well as to the church family. In comparison to early baptism in public places, today's baptismal tanks are located in church buildings and baptisms are performed out of sight of unbelievers which has minimized the importance of the testimonial aspect of the event.

---

[22] Acts 8:36
[23] Ephesians 2:7 NIV
[24] Ephesians 2:8-9 NIV

Baptism is not a bold step in America as it was in the early days of the Church. In fact, today there is little pressure from families to force believers to recant Christianity, except for Jewish or Muslim converts. Therefore, church leadership should not minimize the importance of a public affirmation of one's faith in Jesus as Lord before the saved and unsaved alike. The baptismal step was generally a public affair and took tremendous courage in New Testament times; many lost their lives because they took that step. Baptism doesn't seem to mean much today nor does it have any serious repercussions when one is baptized. Many Christians seem to take a ho-hum attitude towards baptism when, in fact, one's conversion is a miracle and it ought to be recognized as such.

The reality and genuineness of conversion ("a heart affair") was to be validated by identifying with the death and resurrection of Jesus Christ publicly, a courageous and bold step. The crowd who listened to Peter's sermon on the day of Pentecost cried out, "Brethren, what shall we do?" Peter responded, "Repent, and each of you be baptized in the name of Jesus Christ for the forgiveness of your sins; and you will receive the gift of the Holy Spirit."[25]

Baptism was the first order of business after repentance. New converts did not assume the decision was theirs and *they* are the ones who decided whether they wanted to be baptized or not. Certainly our friends in the Churches of Christ have it right when baptism follows conversion closely (but it is not right if anyone teaches that new disciples are not fully saved unless they are baptized). And the longer they put it off, the less they think of it as the "first step of obedience."

However, when believers understand the truth about this "first step" and then outright refuse or procrastinate—assuming it is not important or it can be addressed someday, they enter a state of disobedience.

When any step of obedience is taken, blessings follow.

---

[25] Acts 2:37-38

CAUTION

New believers baptized as babies
must prepare parents and relatives before
they choose to be baptized by immersion,
especially if they have Godparents.
These individuals did what they believed
to be good and should be thanked.

Believer's baptism can be explained to them as
a new step in one's spiritual search for truth.
Show them that the Ephesian believers
(Acts 19) were baptized a second time:
the first time by John the Baptist as they submitted
to his teaching and the second time by Paul
when they expressed their personal belief in
and commitment to the fuller knowledge of
Jesus as Savior and Lord.

CHAPTER 9

BAPTIZED *IN* THE HOLY SPIRIT

The Holy Spirit and the Believer (1)

I

W here does one find in the Bible the expression "baptized in the Holy Spirit"?

The closest expression is found in Acts 1:5, but the phrase there contains the word "with" not "in." True. That text says, "baptized with the Holy Spirit." However, if your Bible has footnotes, check there. The footnotes of popular contemporary versions give the word "in": "baptized in the Holy Spirit."

This chapter and the next two chapters are extremely important for the authentic Christian. They explain the role of the Holy Spirit in the life of the believer. The goal in this chapter is to understand Luke's phrase, baptized with/in the Holy Spirit. In the following two chapters, the goal is to understand Luke's phrase, "filled with the Spirit" in relation to spiritual gifts and spiritual fruit.

However, before we begin, I need to give you fair warning. In this chapter, we will dig deeper to learn the meaning of several words in the original language and we will make a comparison of several texts, noting their similarity of Greek grammar. It will be painless, I assure you, but profitable. Please bear with me. Although not a Greek scholar, I studied New Testament Greek for a couple of years and continued to work with the Greek language for twelve years while doing translation work in West Africa; I would like to offer some of my findings.

But what is Jesus really telling His disciples? Acts 1:5 is our key verse for this chapter. With unusual unanimity among the several popular translations of the English Bible, the translators all use the English preposition "with" twice, once with the word "water" and again with the word "Spirit". The text reads:

> John baptized with water, but you will be baptized with the
> Holy Spirit not many days from now. [1]

The word "with" in this sentence is generic in the sense that it allows various denominations to interpret the method of baptism according to their own beliefs: sprinkling, pouring, or immersion. To use the word "in" rather than "with" would exclude those who practice sprinkling. However, I believe "in" is biblically preferable and I will show that to be true in this chapter so that we may know what Jesus was really telling His disciples.

If "in" is more consistent with cross-references, then Luke is presenting a different role for the Holy Spirit than is generally accorded Him. The challenge is to determine if "in" is correct and if so, the second challenge is to ascertain the biblical meaning of the phrase "in the Spirit". Then we will know what Jesus wants us to know about the role of the Holy Spirit He is sending into the world.

Let's start with this question: Are the two phrases the same grammatically in the original language? I am referring to the phrase, "John baptized with water," and the second phrase in the sentence, "you will be baptized with the Holy Spirit." The answer is yes. The words "water" and "Spirit" are in the same grammatical position. Because of their position in a prepositional phrase, there are three choices the Greek grammar offers for translators to use: by, with, or in.

There are two considerations in determining which word is better: linguistic (i.e., readability) and biblical or theological. We hope one answer can be found that will satisfy both considerations. Here's the text again using "in water" and "in the Holy Spirit":

> John baptized *in water*, but you will be baptized *in the Holy
> Spirit* not many days from now.[2]

Look first for any differences between the two thoughts expressed in Acts 1:5. One difference in the first reference to baptism indicates that John did the baptizing but in the second clause, the baptizer is not mentioned because the

---

[1] Acts 1:5
[2] Acts 1:5

verb is passive. Is the baptizer the Holy Spirit as some assume? The answer is, "No." The baptizer is Jesus Christ, as John the Baptist declared.[3]

Here is yet another observation. Turn to Acts 2, where the Holy Spirit comes down upon the disciples. Luke does not say, "They were baptized with the Spirit" nor does he say, "They were baptized in the Spirit." Rather, Luke says the disciples were "filled with the Spirit." Question: do the words baptized (Acts 1:5) and filled (Acts 2:4) mean the same thing? No, they do not.

"Filled" is much more dramatic and important. Luke leaves it to the reader's imagination to assume that "baptized" and "filled" occurred at the same time. In this moment, the Church was created with charter members equipped to proclaim the Gospel with power. As we define the terms, we will see that "baptized" and "filled" are *not* synonymous.

Here's another difference. In Acts 1:5, we find the phrase "with the Spirit." That same phrase, "with the Spirit," is found in Acts 2:4. They are translated as though they were identical in the original language. They are not. Sorry to be so picky, but serious students are picky and when they find differences they try to find out why the writers of Scripture chose certain words or used particular grammatical constructions. Exact meaning is their goal. That is what we are doing in this chapter.

The grammar of the phrase "with the Spirit" in Acts 1:5 is a prepositional phrase using what is called in Greek the dative case, but the prepositional phrase in Acts 2:4 is *not* the dative case. So, what's the deal? We will examine Acts 2:4 in the next chapter and zero in on Acts 1:5 in this chapter. Our main question for this chapter is this: what does "baptized in the Holy Spirit" mean?

We begin with the word baptize. The English word is actually a transliteration of the Greek word *baptizo*. Let me repeat the definition of the Greek word *baptizo* as found in the lexicon (the Greek dictionary):

1. to dip
2. to immerse, to submerge (used of boats sunk in the water)
3. to cleanse by dipping or submerging, to wash, to make clean with water, to wash one's self, to bathe

---

[3] The Greek language is very rich and very complex; there are five possible endings to nouns, called case endings. A dative case ending may be understood as instrumental or locative. For example: I-baptized-you-water. The noun water might be used as an instrumental dative, indicating what was used to perform the baptism: "I baptized you *with water*." But it could also be a locative dative, indicating where the baptism took place: "I baptized you *in water*" (Mark 1:8). However, since the core meaning of the verb is "immerse," the dative is likely locative and means "in water."

4. to overwhelm

John called on Israel to repent of their sins and when they repented, he baptized them and it is quite conceivable that, given the definition of baptize, he immersed his followers. The teachers of the day baptized their converts as well. Even the Jews baptized converts to Judaism.[4] They saw it as purification.

John's baptism in water demonstrated symbolically the washing away of sins. His baptismal candidates announced to the Israelite community by their baptism that they had a heart change and were now disciples of John. They were identifying with John's message and preparing for the coming Messiah. Repenting, they placed themselves under John's authority. Jesus followed the practice of the day but three years later, Jesus also promised His disciples a spiritual baptism.

As just noted, Luke doesn't mention the fulfillment of Jesus' promise of a spiritual baptism that was made to the disciples in Acts 1:5, but their baptism certainly occurred as Jesus prophesied, "in a few days," since, on Pentecost, they received power to testify. This is what Jesus promised and because of it, His disciples' lives were dramatically changed. As a result of the filling of the Spirit, the disciples were gifted with the ability to speak a multitude of foreign languages and explain the Gospel to thousands of foreign-born Jews who dwelled (i.e., settled) in Jerusalem and still remembered their mother tongue.

This spiritual baptism affirmed the disciples' commitment to Jesus as Savior and Lord. It was not a visible or external event but the results were. In one sense, it was an aural event for the disciples; everyone heard the sound of the coming of the Spirit. This immersion in the Spirit was no less real than the immersion in water of John the Baptist's baptism.

II

In Acts 1, it is obvious that Jesus was not talking about water baptism. That would have happened at a prior time. We are not told when Jesus baptized the twelve disciples with water, but since it was the habit of teachers

---

[4] The Amora'im who produced the Talmud set out three requirements for a conversion to Judaism (Keritot 8b), which must be witnessed and affirmed by a rabbinical court composed of three Jewish males above the age of thirteen (they do not need to be rabbis). (1) Circumcision, (2) Offering a certain sacrifice (*korban*) in the Temple, and (3) Immersion (*tevelah*) in a ritual bath for both men and women. Retrieved from https://en.wikipedia.org/wiki/Conversion_to_Judaism.

of that day to baptize their converts at their calling, we can believe He baptized them. Then it was a common practice to allow their first converts to baptize those who came later. The Apostle John makes a comment that, although a little ambiguous, seems to imply the disciples' baptism in water.

> After these things Jesus and His disciples came into the land of Judea, and there He was spending time with them and baptizing.[5]

Some argue that John the Baptist baptized the disciples and that sufficed. Let me reiterate that it was the practice of the teachers of the day to baptize their disciples. There is no reason to believe Jesus would not have done the same to authenticate the twelve men who stayed with Him as His disciples. The Pharisees', John's, and Jesus' disciples are pointed out as different groups by Mark in his Gospel.[6]

Now we will look further into the question: were they "baptized *with* the Holy Spirit" or "baptized *in* the Holy Spirit" or even a third possibility, "baptized *by* the Holy Spirit"? As noted above, the Greek permits all three possibilities. The translators of the popular versions of the Bible for the most part chose "with" using "in" as a footnote. David Guzik explains spiritual baptism in his "Study Guide for Acts 1" and he favors "in":

> The idea of being baptized is to be immersed or covered over in something; even as John baptized people in water, so these disciples would be "immersed" in the Holy Spirit.
>
> Perhaps it is more useful to describe the baptism of the Holy Spirit more like a *condition* than an *experience*. We should perhaps ask, "*are you* baptized in the Holy Spirit [your condition]?" "instead of asking, "*have you been* baptized in the Holy Spirit [your experience]?"

Ellicott in his Commentary for English Readers uses the word plunge to explain this concept. This is what he writes: "Now they were told that their spirits were to be as fully baptized, i.e., plunged, into the power of the Divine Spirit, as their bodies had then been plunged in the waters of the Jordan."

---

[5] John 3:22

[6] Mark 2:18, John's disciples and the Pharisees were fasting; and they came and said to Him, "Why do John's disciples and the disciples of the Pharisees fast, but your disciples do not fast?"

I submit that when "with the Spirit" is compared with other phrases that are grammatically identical, "in" is more appropriate and therefore a true biblical solution. Ellicott has provided us with the precise meaning. Let me explain further.

If the word should be "in" instead of "with," that raises an interesting question. We can visualize someone being baptized in the water of the Jordan River. But how does one visualize someone being immersed *in* the Holy Spirit? We cannot since it is a spiritual condition that allows the Holy Spirit to make dead spirits come alive and in which He takes up residence. A believer's dead spirit comes alive because of faith in Jesus as Savior and Lord, and Jesus baptizes this new believer by immersing him or her in the Holy Spirit. That makes the believer a "new creation" like the cucumber transformed into a pickle by having been immersed in vinegar. For the new believer, the event is called regeneration, meaning, of course, born again.

The Holy Spirit now lives within the new believer and he or she needs to submit to the voice of the Spirit. The Holy Spirit then waits for an invitation to enter the mind and houseclean. The goal is to purify the mind and instruct in godly behavior. Sometimes the process is painful but its final result is always blessing. That's the sanctification process explained by the Apostle Paul in Romans 12:1-2. Check the chapter on Salvation-Sanctification.

III

Comparing Scripture with Scripture to see what Luke is really saying in Acts 1:5, we find there are three identical examples of grammar where the word "baptized" is used along with two identical Greek prepositions. Those prepositions are: *eis* (in, into) and *en* (in). In each case, the second Greek word (*en*) is followed by a Greek dative case noun and can be translated by a prepositional phrase that begins with by, in, or with depending on the context. See the box.

> They were baptized into [eis] Moses
> in [en*] the cloud and the sea.
> 1 Corinthians 10:2
> They were baptized into [eis] John
> in [en*] the Jordan (river).
> Acts 19:3 with Mark 1:5
> We are baptized into [eis] Christ
> in [en*] the Holy Spirit.
> Romans 6:3 with Acts 1:5
> (*introduces the dative case)

Do you see the similarities? The two little prepositions in brackets hold the clue for understanding the role the Holy Spirit plays in the believer's spiritual baptism. The first, *eis,* means *in* or *into,* and the second, *en,* also means "in." The difference is this: the first word, *eis,* implies going into something, a house for example. In this text, it is used to speak of commitment to ("going into") the teaching of Moses, John, or Jesus. Or, we might say, they "stepped into it."

The second, *en,* indicates one is *in* or *inside* the house. One is *enveloped* by the house might be another way of looking at it. Is our whole personality immersed in the Spirit as well as our spirit? The answer is no because that does not happen until we "present ourselves a living sacrifice," as Paul urges in Romans 12:1. It is then that the Holy Spirit has the privilege of doing that work. When He is invited into the believer's mind, with the cooperation of the believer, He will change the believer's personality one value at a time to conform to the likeness of Christ. The initial commitment of "Take all of me, Lord" requires an act of our will, and is often a second crisis occurring sometime after the initial crisis of regeneration. A fuller explanation is found in the next chapter.

Perhaps the following will help clarify the difference between *eis* and *en* and help make the role of the Holy Spirit in a believer's life better understood. Let's examine the parallels one at a time, first the text about Moses, then John, and finally Jesus (this is the same pattern).

Summary Statements

1. 1 Corinthians 10:2 – "they were baptized into [eis] Moses in [en] the cloud and the sea"

125

"Baptized into [eis]" indicates identification with and submission to Moses and his teaching. The word baptizo is used to describe the process. The second word, en, indicates the means whereby this was accomplished.

2. Compare Acts 19:3 with Mark 1:5 – the Ephesians were baptized "into [eis] John in [en] the Jordan"

    John the Baptist's disciples publicly identified themselves as disciples of God's servant, John the Baptist, by permitting him to baptize them. They placed themselves under John (eis), recognizing him as their teacher. The means used to accomplish their affirmation was external. They were baptized "in (en) the Jordan River." The river was the medium or agent in which the baptism took place.

3. Compare Romans 6:3 with Acts 1:5 – "We are baptized into [eis] Christ…in [en] the Holy Spirit."

    Christians "step into" the teachings of Christ (eis) and are immersed in the Holy Spirit. How does that happen? That's a question whose answer will be found in Heaven; here on earth, we do not know. It is a spiritual work that is the responsibility of the Holy Spirit. When does it happen? That's a question that can be answered with some degree of certainty. John 3:16 assures "the world" that the one who believes in Jesus Christ—in the atoning work He has done on the cross and the fact that He arose from the dead—that one receives "life everlasting." And life everlasting is spiritual life; it is the work of God the Holy Spirit and is only possible through a divine act of God.

4. As to John's words, "baptized with the Holy Spirit," using "in" rather than "with" presents a better picture: the disciples were to be "baptized in the Holy Spirit," that is, their dead spirits were to be immersed in the Holy Spirit to become alive. The human spirit that has been made alive is able to communicate personally with God and He with them. The translation using "in" parallels the Greek phrases, "in the Jordan" and "in the cloud and the sea." If John practiced immersion—and I think he did—every part of the candidate was wet from the water. Keep that picture in mind as we continue to examine the evidence of Jesus baptizing His disciples in the Holy

Spirit. A definite change occurred in the life of the disciples. They immediately went out proclaiming the Gospel!

It is difficult for Gentiles to appreciate the tremendous impact Paul's teaching had on the Jews. They surely were astonished at the broad reach of the Gospel:

For by one Spirit we were all baptized into one body, whether Jews or Greeks, whether slaves or free, and we were all made to drink of one Spirit.

I am trying to make clear that a believer's baptism is not "the Holy Spirit's baptism." Nor are believers baptized into the Holy Spirit. No, the Scriptures are clear that believers are baptized "into Christ," that is, into Christ's Body which is the Church Universal. Believers have the divine privilege of being immersed in the Holy Spirit as a witness to their faith.

Picture a believer being enveloped in the Holy Spirit during his or her spiritual baptism. More than that, one's spirit is fully saturated with the Holy Spirit and he or she is now alive spiritually because of the new birth. Also, due to the new birth, a believer is now a possessor of eternal life. This baptism enables the believer to be ready for service (gifts of the Spirit are given to a believer who faithfully proclaims the Gospel), and ready for character development (fruit of the Spirit is developed in any believer who is willing to listen to the voice of the Spirit). "Gifts of the Spirit" is the subject of the Chapter 10 and "Fruit of the Spirit" the subject of Chapter 11.

What is needed is to welcome the Holy Spirit into one's soul (mind, emotions, and personality) and give Him permission to do housecleaning. He will begin the process, pointing out those issues where one "continues to be conformed to this world"[7] and He will help you, the believer, to continue to "be transformed by the renewing of your mind."[8] The exciting news follows: "Then you will be able to test and approve what God's will is—his good, pleasing and perfect will."[9]

The Holy Spirit does not bring us a body of teaching more complete than that given to us by Jesus. To believe that is heresy! Jesus' message relative to regeneration, sanctification, and glorification is complete. The Holy Spirit's role is to provide understanding of all that Jesus taught and in addition, to

---

[7] Romans 12:2
[8] Ibid.
[9] Ibid.

give power to assist believers in accomplishing the Lord's work. That's when the Spirit's gifts are important.

Jesus said that when the Holy Spirit came upon His disciples and was abiding within them, the Holy Spirit, would bring to their remembrance everything that He, Jesus, had said to them. In addition, Jesus said the Spirit would not speak of Himself.[10]

Today, "baptism in the Spirit" occurs at regeneration; it is then that a Christian's spirit is made alive and he or she receives the gift of everlasting life. The evidence is a life filled with the desire to change for the better, a desire to do the will of God, and a desire to share the Good News. If Christians are already "baptized in the Spirit," why don't we see new believers speaking in tongues? Good question and that is addressed in the next chapter. A more important question is this: if Christians are baptized in the Holy Spirit at regeneration, why don't we see more Christ-like Christians in our neighborhoods and in our workplaces?

Some sincere Christians are unsettled because they feel they are missing some special relationship with the Holy Spirit. Generally that occurs because they are aware of our charismatic brothers and sisters who believe that one must speak in tongues to be fulfilled. And these dear folk are warm-hearted and joyful.

To be fulfilled as a Christian, we must love God with our whole being and our neighbor as we love ourselves. This is what Christians need to be concerned about! The Holy Spirit has been given to believers to help them do just that. Who doesn't need help to implement that most basic of truths? It's the Holy Spirit who, Jesus said, is the Helper we've been given.[11]

Let me say it again. Since the Church has been brought into being, those converted after Pentecost are immediately made alive spiritually and put into the Body of Christ (the Church). That is realized because the Holy Spirit immerses the one who exercises faith in the atoning work of Jesus Christ. A changing character and spiritual empowering are. the proof of a spiritual baptism. As the believer serves the Body and reaches out to the world, further evidence is the gift(s) the Holy Spirit gives to assist the believer in the proclamation of the Gospel.

---

[10] John 16:13-14
[11] John 16:7

The Spirit is ready to help with interpretation and application of all that Jesus taught but the believer must be willing to study the Word diligently as Paul points out to Timothy:

> Be diligent to present yourself approved to God as a workman who does not need to be ashamed, accurately handling the word of truth.

The Holy Spirit is ready to equip believers to live a Christlike life and proclaim the Gospel of Jesus Christ without hypocrisy. And He is ready to give whatever miraculous gift is necessary to confirm the Word spoken by a believer.

I repeat: contemporary Christians are *baptized in the Spirit* at their second birth (regeneration) and at that time, are made a part of the "Body of Christ."

If that statement is true (and I believe it is) you may wonder why there isn't more evidence of spiritual gifts and spiritual fruit. That's a good question and we will find some answers as we examine the phrase in Acts 2:4, "*filled with the Spirit.*" That is the subject of the next chapter.

Since the understanding about being *baptized in the Spirit* is so misunderstood by many and is new to others, I have tried to present the material with some repetition. I trust you can pray the following prayer.

> Thank you, Holy Spirit,
> for letting my dead spirit
> be immersed in your Spirit,
> and making me alive in my spirit.
> I was dead but now I truly live!
> Holy Spirit, help me understand
> the profound truths Jesus taught.
> Thank you.
> Amen.

CHAPTER 10

FILLED WITH THE SPIRIT - *GIFTS*

The Holy Spirit and the Believer (2)

I

In this lesson, we will see the newborn Church come into being and God's method of empowering it.

Before Jesus ascended into Heaven, He promised His disciples they would be *baptized in the Holy Spirit* and when the Holy Spirit came upon them, Jesus also promised they would receive *power*. In Acts 2, that promise was fulfilled and at the same time, they began to exalt the Messiah, Jesus Christ, in many languages that were the mother tongues of the crowd gathering around them. This initial filling is found in Acts 2:4. There we read:

> And they were all filled with the Holy Spirit and began to speak with other tongues, as the Spirit was giving them utterance.

The word for 'tongues'—as in English—is a synonym for 'language' and those languages recorded in Acts 2 were known languages found in communities from Mesopotamia in the east to the rim of the Mediterranean to the west. Tongues was the first expressions of power received from the Holy Spirit but the Apostle Paul refers to the availability of many other gifts of the Spirit bestowed on the new entity that God created on that feast day called Pentecost.

Paul wrote to the Corinthians and explained the purpose of the gifts, *"But to each one is given the manifestation of the Spirit for the common good."*[1] Who is going to determine *'the common good?'* Note the control the Holy Spirit exercises: *"But one and the same Spirit works all these things, distributing to each one individually just as He wills."*[2]

Be aware that every believer has been given a gift. What gift? Get busy serving the Lord and you will be surprised at the feedback you will receive from others who tend to recognize another believer's gift first before recognizing his or her own.

Why did the Holy Spirit choose to empower the disciples first with the gift of tongues? Paul clarifies that issue in his first letter to the Corinthians. In Chapter 14, he shows his concern about disorder in the church over which gift, tongues or prophecy, should be preeminent in the church service. He explains why tongues is given and why prophecy is given:

> So then tongues are for a sign, not to those who believe but
> to unbelievers; but prophecy is for a sign, not to unbelievers
> but to those who believe.[3]

It is the Spirit who determines who gets what gift. But doesn't Paul say, *"Desire the best gifts?"* Yes, He does at the conclusion of his chapter on love.[4] However, whatever believers desire must be in accord with the will of God and who better to enable the believer to be knowledgeable of God's will than the Spirit of God? And if one wants to know the will of God, the process is laid out clearly in Romans 12:1-2.

There are three reasons why tongues (or, languages) was the first gift the Holy Spirit gave to the newborn Church.

1. The gift enabled the disciples to reach out to Jerusalem, the first location on their agenda.

2. The gift enabled the foreign-born, 'devout,' unprejudiced Jews living in Jerusalem to find their Messiah.

3. The gift was the fulfillment of an Old Testament prophecy:

---

[1] 1 Corinthians 12:7
[2] Ibid.
[3] 1 Corinthians 14:22
[4] 1 Corinthians 13

In the Law it is written, "By men of strange tongues and by the lips of strangers I will speak to this people, and even so they will not listen to Me," says the Lord.[5]

During that Old Testament period, the Jews were rebellious to their God and their worship was increasingly unacceptable. God warned them that if they didn't repent and follow the revealed Law, He would accept worship from those who spoke foreign languages. Be sure the Jews thought that would never happen since they were persuaded Jehovah was Israel's God and of course only spoke Hebrew. How much more rebellious could they get than to crucify His Son?

Ten days after Christ's ascension, God spoke through the disciples in the mother tongue of the people groups listed in Acts 2. These were the foreign languages God promised would happen. At a later date, many more 'foreigners' praised God including the Samaritans, the Gentiles in Caesarea, and the Ephesians. The Jews living in those four places would have studied the Old Testament Scriptures and would have known the prophecy. They, too, would have heard the astounding fulfillment of that promise since, as boys, they studied with the rabbis and memorized much of the Old Testament. They had to be amazed!

The unprejudiced Jews opened their hearts and received the truth; those who were prejudiced continued to harden their hearts. Therefore, knowing what the Scriptures say about the Pharisees and Sadducees—and their low view of Nazareth—it can safely be said that they had a low view of the disciples' new converts who were praising God in their mother tongue. They would have seen them as second-class, Johnny-come-lately Jews who were born in ungodly countries, growing up among ungodly people, speaking the languages of the ungodly.

Some commentaries suggest the crowds were travelers from every known nation coming to Jerusalem for the celebrations of Firstfruits and Shavuot (Pentecost)—and many did just that. However, there is a surprise embedded in Luke's writing that doesn't appear in our English translation. Luke's choice of a particular expression explains who they were. Examine the phrase, 'living in Jerusalem" found in Acts 2:5, "Now there were Jews living in Jerusalem, devout men from every nation under heaven."

It's the word '*living*' that is the clue. The Greek word tells us these people 'dwelled in Jerusalem,' that is, they had taken up *permanent residence*

---

[5] 1 Corinthians 14:21

in Jerusalem. Were there also some in the crowd who traveled to Jerusalem because the buzz was that it was time for the Messiah to appear? Probably. Were some there because they had come to Jerusalem to learn Hebrew? Probably. Were some there just to celebrate the holy days? Yes. And probably some were there to visit relatives. The crowd around the disciples was different. They were immigrants who came to learn more about the expected Messiah and they were not disappointed. They would know some Hebrew, especially enough to allow them to share meaningfully in Temple worship. However, without doubt, they spoke it with an accent since Hebrew was not their mother tongue. The native-born leaders in Jerusalem were the purists and they would have discriminated against the immigrants.

God steered these immigrants clear of entrapment in legalistic Judaism. These were truth-seekers and God, seeing their heart's desire, opened their spiritual eyes to see even more clearly that Jesus of Nazareth was the Messiah. And God used them to fulfill prophecy concerning His Son.

II

What are the gifts of the Spirit?

Here is the list of gifts Paul gave to the Corinthians. Please note that "word of wisdom" and "word of knowledge" are at the head of Paul's list. "Prophecy" is number six and "tongues" and "interpretation of tongues" are at the bottom. Jewish writers seem to put the item of greatest importance first, making their first words sound like a newspapers headline.

> For to one is given the word of wisdom through the Spirit,
>
> and to another the word of knowledge according to the same Spirit;
>
> to another faith by the same Spirit,
>
> and to another gifts of healing by the one Spirit,
>
> and to another the effecting of miracles,
>
> and to another prophecy,
>
> and to another the distinguishing of spirits,
>
> to another various kinds of tongues,

and to another the interpretation of tongues.[6]

Paul also gave a list to the Romans. This list is different but should be viewed as complementary. Paul wrote:

> Since we have gifts that differ according to the grace given to us, each of us is to exercise them accordingly:
>
> if prophecy, according to the proportion of his faith;
>
> service, in his serving;
>
> he who teaches, in his teaching;
>
> or he who exhorts, in his exhortation;
>
> he who gives, with liberality;
>
> he who leads, with diligence;
>
> who shows mercy, with cheerfulness.[7]

Paul emphasized the fact that not everyone has the same gift. No doubt there was contention within the church body over which was the more important, prophecy or tongues. Here's what he said:

> God has appointed in the church, first apostles, second prophets, third teachers, then miracles, then gifts of healings, helps, administrations, various kinds of tongues. All are not apostles, are they? All are not prophets, are they? All are not teachers, are they? All are not workers of miracles, are they? All do not have gifts of healings, do they? All do not speak with tongues, do they? All do not interpret, do they?[8]

In 1 Corinthians 12, Paul reminded his readers of the analogy of the body and the interdependence of the individual parts of the body. He closed the section by shifting his argument to a whole new level; he wanted to show them a new approach. He explained, "But earnestly desire the greater gifts. And I show you a still more excellent way." [9]

Paul launched into his "more excellent way" in the next chapter. Chapter 13 is a beautiful discourse on love and love is "the more excellent way."

---

[6] 1 Corinthians 12:8-10
[7] Romans 12:6-8
[8] 1 Corinthians 12:28
[9] 1 Corinthians 12:31

Paul wrote to the Ephesian church and gave a list of gifts that differs yet again, but these gifts are offices for the church.

And He [Christ] gave some as apostles,

and some as prophets,

and some as evangelists,

and some as pastors and teachers (or, pastor-teachers).[10]

As to the purpose of these office gifts, Paul was specific when he said they are "for the equipping of the saints for the work of service, to the building up the body of Christ."[11] For those who want to bypass leadership and authority, they reject God who created these offices to provide teaching, order, and security for the church.

Did the office of the apostles cease with the Twelve (i.e., the Eleven plus Matthias)? That's the general opinion held by many. The Twelve are very special and ought to be written with a capital "T" but there were others referred to by the same Greek word, *apostolos* which means, 'sent one.' Jesus sent them "into all the world" hence this descriptive title. Examples include: Barnabas (Acts 14:14) and Paul (Romans 1:1).

What are we to make of the several lists called gifts? First, I would say, do not limit the Spirit of God. Second, expect whatever He believes is best for any given situation, and third, don't be surprised at the Spirit's ingenuity.

III

Luke who wrote the Gospel that bears his name and the book of Acts has some delightful surprises in store for the diligent student of the Word. For those who dig deeper, there are rich rewards because his Greek is more precise than our English versions indicate.

The first surprise for English readers was Luke's inspired phrase in Chapter 1, to be understood not as baptized with the Spirit, but baptized in the Spirit. We examined that in the previous chapter and found that at conversion (regeneration), our spirit is immersed in the Holy Spirit just as John the Baptist immersed his disciples in water. As a result, believers are made alive spiritually for evermore!

---

[10] Ephesians 4:11
[11] Ephesians 4:12

The second surprise is the fact that Luke quotes Jesus as promising His disciples they would be baptized in the Spirit but doesn't mention their baptism again as a separate event in the exciting chapter that follows. Obviously, Luke took for granted his contemporaries would understand that when the disciples were filled with the Spirit (Chapter 2), they would also be baptized in the Spirit (promised in Chapter 1). When filled, they manifested a spiritual gift; this was confirmation they were baptized and bona fide disciples of Jesus Christ. "Filling" is the important issue for Luke in the book of Acts.

Let me emphasize again that when one accepts the substitutionary death of Christ on the cross—meaning He died in place of sinners and paid the penalty for their sins—that person's spirit is made alive and communication is restored between the new believer and God. Paul calls the new believer "a new creation."[12] Therefore, as a result of the four-fold appearance of the Holy Spirit—in Jerusalem, Samaria, Caesarea, and Ephesus—each group of new believers manifested the same gift of power (tongues) and unity prevailed in the newly formed Church.[13]

The signs of the filling are the gifts of the Holy Spirit (this lesson) and the fruit of the Holy Spirit that show a change in lifestyle (next lesson). The Holy Spirit came to exalt Christ; Christ did not send the Holy Spirit so the Spirit would exalt Himself. Predicting the coming of the Spirit, Jesus said:

> When the Helper comes, whom I will send to you from the Father, that is the Spirit of truth who proceeds from the Father, He will testify about Me.[14]

The third surprise for English readers is in Acts 2:4 and will be of interest to those who look for the finer points in grammar. The prepositional phrase in verse four is with the Spirit and one would naturally compare it with the same phrase (in English) that is found in Acts 1:5, with the Spirit. But these phrases are not the same grammatical construction in Greek. In Acts 1:5, Spirit is an indirect object answering the question "how?" and speaks of the means by which something is done. Acts 1:5 can read, immersed in the Spirit.

In Acts 2:4, Spirit is a direct object limiting the action of the verb "filled" to the disciples. The direct object answers 'what?' or 'who'. The translation for the phrase in Acts 2:4 is with the Spirit and that is a good translation. God's

---

[12] 2 Corinthians 5:17
[13] See Acts 15
[14] John 15:26

servants are finally empowered to do God's work by the Spirit's filling. What a blessing for the Church as it begins its mission!

Read Acts 2:2-4 and note the Greek word I inserted following the two words 'filled' and you will find a fourth surprise: the words are different in Greek although the translation is the same in English (See box below).

> When the day of Pentecost had come, they were all
> together in one place. And suddenly there came from
> heaven a noise like a violent rushing wind, and it filled
> [*pléroö*] the whole house where they were sitting.
> And there appeared to them tongues as
> of fire distributing themselves,
> and they rested on each one of them.
> And they were all filled [*plétho*] with the Holy Spirit and
> began to speak with other tongues, as the
> Spirit was giving them utterance.

Luke was an educated man and quite particular in his use of these two different words for 'fill' as a search of the Gospel of Luke and the book of Acts reveals. We'll look at the definition of these two terms, but first, there is something else awaiting the diligent student of the Word (see the box below).

> HEADS UP FOR ANOTHER SURPRISE
> The Greek word for "filled" in Acts 2:4
> is different from the word for "filled"
> found in Acts 2:2 and Ephesians 5:18.

Definitions

1. 'Filled' in Acts 2:2 and Ephesians 5:18 — the Greek word is *pléroö* (discussed in the next lesson). The meaning of the word is simply, "to fill (where empty)" or "to fill up to the top." The English word 'filled' is an adequate translation.[15]

---

[15] Merriam-Webster gives the following as one definition for this meaning of "fill," as to occupy the whole of, <smoke *filled* the room.> In Acts 2:2, the sound was heard throughout the house!

2. 'Filled' in Acts 2:4 — the Greek word is *plétho* (discussed in this lesson). The meaning of the word implies more than just 'fill.' The phrase is found in Acts 2:4, which states "they were all filled [*plétho*] with the Holy Spirit and began to speak with other tongues."

Plétho and *pléroö* have the same root but different suffixes. A study of the contexts indicates both words means 'fill' but *plétho* carries an implication not found in *pléroö*. Here's how *plétho* is used in the New Testament:

> ➤ *plétho* means 'fill, filled to the brim,' and is used of things: for example, Luke 5:7, boats were (dangerously) filled with fish; Matthew 27:48, a sponge was filled with vinegar (saturated); Acts 19:29, a city was filled (with confusion); Matthew 22:10; a wedding reception was filled (wall-to-wall) with guests

> ➤ *plétho* is used of people by Luke, especially in relation to their empowerment with spiritual gifts. The disciples were filled (*plétho*) with the Holy Spirit according to passages in Luke and Acts (Luke 1:15, 41, 67; Acts 2:4; 4:8 and 31; 9: 17; and 13:9)

> ➤ *plétho is* used when people were filled and express strong feelings to the point of being irrational

What the various examples show is that in usage, *plétho* seems to indicate filling to the brim and being controlled by that with which it is filled. In English, we could use the example, "He lost his head and swore profusely."[16]

Luke was so careful to use *plétho* in Luke 5:7, while he used *pléroö* for the boat that was about to be swamped by wind and waves in Luke 8:23. The Luke 5:7 passage tells of an incident about fish and it reads:

And [their partners] came and filled [*plétho*] both of the boats [with fish], so that they began to sink.

The Luke 8:23 passage reads:

But as they sailed He fell asleep. And a windstorm came down on the lake, and they were filling [*pléroö*] with water, and were in jeopardy.[17]

The verb *plétho* (5:7) indicates the weight of the fish controlled the boat in Luke five as Luke explains in the tag that he adds: *filled (with fish)… was about*

---

[16] The word *plétho* can also mean "complete."
[17] New King James Version, NKJV

to sink whereas in Luke 8:23, the wind and waves did not yet have control of the boat; the men still did. The situation was getting tense, however, and the seasoned fisherman saw the boat *filling [pléroö] with water* and knew this called for action on their part to avoid a dangerous filling [*plétho*]. Since they could see the situation was getting out of hand, it was 'all hands on deck' as they say, and they awakened the Master and enlisted His help. To their amazement, He didn't grab an oar to help; He stood up and "rebuked the wind and the surging waves, and they stopped and it became calm."

We can also envision an unpleasant sponge *filled [saturated] with vinegar.* Since it, being a sponge, sopped up the vinegar, an acrid smell and biting taste would have prevailed.

Emotions are paired with the verb "filled [*plétho*]" and in doing so the implication is that they were controlled by the emotion. The emotions in the Scriptures include fear, madness, wonder, jealousy and envy. We understand that when these emotions gripped individuals, they became totally caught up in them and were no longer thinking clearly.

Were the disciples irrational when the Holy Spirit came upon them and controlled their speaking apparatus in order to get the Word out and fulfill prophecy? No! The power of the Holy Spirit gripped them but this was not an emotional thing! This welled up from their renewed spirits, not from their emotions. There's a big difference! This spiritual event was quite a witness to the crowds who gathered.

Later, Peter reported to the Jerusalem church that the Gentiles in Caesarea and the Samaritans in Samaria received the Holy Spirit just as they did in Jerusalem and the result was the same: the gift of tongues. That was a happy development because it promoted unity. Since Peter says what happened among the Gentiles in both these locations was the same as happened in Jerusalem, he is saying the tongues spoken in those places were also known languages. Evidently there were immigrants in those locations and that is not hard to imagine given the roads built by the Romans and the deployment everywhere of Roman soldiers to keep the peace,

Why is this phenomenon of tongues important? As noted earlier, the Apostle Paul quoted one of the prophets who warned Israel that the unthinkable was going to happen because of their idolatry and rebellion. One day they would hear foreigners exalting and praising Israel's God since Israel would not.

Paul wrote to the Corinthian church that was beset with disunity problems, especially over the issue of two gifts of the Spirit, prophecy and tongues. He spelled out for them, very clearly in Chapter 13, that if he had the gifts of prophecy, knowledge of mysteries, all knowledge, and faith, and if he spoke with eloquence like the transients who gave lectures—yet didn't have love, he had nothing.

Paul then returns to the subject of the controversy surrounding the use of gifts in Chapter 14. Please note in passing that Chapters 12, 13, and 14 are related; read them as a unit. This is how 1 Corinthians 14 begins: "Pursue love, yet desire earnestly spiritual gifts, but especially that you may prophesy."

There was a problem in the church at Corinth; their meetings were characterized by disorder. Paul tackles that problem in Chapter 14. The Holy Spirit gifted the members of the church at Corinth, and prominent were the gifts of tongues and prophesy. They were vying to use their gift in the assembly when they met together for worship. Paul explains why the gift of prophecy is better for the assembly: everyone can understand what is being said whereas that is not the case with tongues.

There was disorder in the meetings because of misunderstanding the purpose of gifts and the public use of them. There was disorder with regards to the behavior of those who attempted to share insights from the word, those who spoke in tongues, and the unspecified behavior of the women present in the meetings. Paul does not prohibit the orderly use of tongues or prophecy or the involvement of both men and women in the service.[18] Rather, Paul says all things must be done for edification of the believers gathered together and 'all things must be done properly and in an orderly manner."[19] Here again is Paul's verse on usage of tongues and prophecy:

> Tongues, then, are a sign, not for believers but for unbelievers; prophecy, however, is not for unbelievers but for believers.[20]

IV

I hope I didn't lose you along the way but in case I did, let me recap and fill in some of the gaps. Some might ask, "What difference does it make?" I will answer that question as we proceed.

---

[18] Philip's daughters were known to prophesy, Acts 21:8-9
[19] I Corinthians 14:40
[20] I Corinthians 14:22

1. The word 'fill' in Acts 2:2 (*the house was filled*) and in Ephesians 5:18 (*Be filled with the Spirit*) are both the same Greek word for 'fill' (*pleroö*) meaning 'fill up' where empty.

   The tense of the verb 'fill' in Ephesians 5:18 and the participles that follow (the -ing words) are all present tense, meaning habitual, or continual action.

   Yes, there are many fillings as the Spirit challenges believers to love God and neighbor more and more.

   The next chapter in Ephesians is devoted to the application of this 'filling' for the Christian life.

2. The second word "filled" is found in Acts 2:4. That word is a different Greek word and in our English translations the phrase reads, "they were all filled with the Spirit." This word carries the idea of what fills, controls. Luke used this word to describe a boat so full of fish that the weight put it perilously close to sinking.

   This filling is evidenced by spiritual gifts; the first was tongues that allowed the newborn Church to have its first evangelistic rally. Other gifts of the Spirit were manifested as the Church matured.

   When a believer responds positively to Romans 12:1 and 2, and then witnesses to an unbeliever, the Holy Spirit may inject a word in the conversation that flows off the believer's tongue. This word will be exactly what the one listening needs. Or, the Holy Spirit may take charge of a believer's entire conversation. Those are filling (*plétho*) events thanks to the Holy Spirit. They may also be repeated as the need arises.

As a believer, did you ever try to help or comfort someone but had no idea what to say? You asked the Lord to help you say something meaningful. Later you learned that what you said was just the right thing. That's the Spirit filling you with the gift of knowledge.

Review the lists below and note especially that wisdom and knowledge are number one and number two on the Apostle Paul's list of spiritual gifts in 1 Corinthians 12:8-10.

1. wisdom

2. knowledge

3. faith

4. gifts of healing

5. miracles

6. prophecy

7. distinguishing of spirits

8. kinds of tongues

9. interpretation of tongues

Here's a second example. I was in my automobile heading in a particular direction to make a house call. I found the house, and discovered no one was home. As I drove back to my office, I asked the Lord if there was something else I could do while I was in that section of town. It suddenly dawned on me—put another way, the Spirit prompted me—that I wasn't too far from another couple who were new to our congregation. And there I was at the junction where I could turn left and visit them.

I had never been there before but I found the house, parked the car, got out and walked up the steps wondering what I would find. Going to the door, I rang the bell. The door opened and the lady of the house took one look at me and said, "The Lord sent you!" And indeed He did! She invited me to step in and be seated. She then related a problem she was facing. We talked about it, had prayer and I left blessing the Lord. She also was blessing the Lord for my coming just at the right time, she said.

Those who are godly are being directed by the Spirit as often as they are open to direction. When godly people have a question to resolve, a word to share with an unbeliever, or they need direction for their own lives, the Holy Spirit provides the guidance, just as Jesus promised.[21]

Have you experienced the blessing of the gifts of the Holy Spirit? If you are a believer, the Scripture says you should desire the best—and that means a gift that is the best for your ministry, not one you think will enhance your personality or look good on your résumé. Then leave the rest to the omniscient and omnipotent Spirit of God who resides within you.

---

[21] John 16:13

James M. Riccitelli

CHAPTER 11

FILLED WITH THE SPIRIT - *FRUIT*

The Holy Spirit and the Believer (3)

I

There is a second function attributable to the Holy Spirit and that is producing spiritual fruit in the life of the believer.

The Holy Spirit baptizes new believers at conversion—that is, at regeneration. Once committed to serving the Lord and baptized in the Spirit, the believer can expect two things to occur in his or her life: empowerment with the Spirit's gifts (Chapter 10), and character changes by means of the Spirit's fruit (this chapter).

On the day of Pentecost, the disciples were filled *(plétho)* with the Holy Spirit. He took control of their vocal apparatus and miraculously enabled them to share the Good News about Jesus Christ in the mother tongues of hundreds of people who began to mill about outside.

The Bible is full of 'miracle stories' and Acts 2 tells of two miracles in verse four: the disciples were immersed in the Holy Spirit and He filled them with Himself and power. That's exactly what Jesus had promised. That's the first miracle. They then spoke in the mother tongues of the immigrants who, hearing the noise of the Spirit's descent, came running to see what was going on. The second miracle is the gift of foreign languages spoken by the disciples.

In the book of Acts, there are additional instances of the disciples being filled with and controlled by the Holy Spirit that resulted in the demonstration of different kinds of gifts for ministry, for example, boldness, visions, casting out demons, and healings. "I believe in miracles," as the hymn says, and I take the Scriptures at face value.

In this chapter, we will examine a different kind of ministry provided by the Holy Spirit. When one is filled with the Holy Spirit, the Spirit will assist the believer in establishing an intimate relationship with the Lord Jesus who said:

> I am the vine, you are the branches. He who abides in Me, and I in him, bears much fruit; for without Me you can do nothing. [1]

The Apostle Paul explains what that fruit is when he writes to the Galatians:

> But the fruit of the Spirit is love, joy, peace, patience, kindness, goodness, faithfulness, gentleness, self-control; against such things there is no law.
>
> Now those who belong to Christ Jesus have crucified the flesh with its passions and desires. If we live by the Spirit, let us also walk by the Spirit. Let us not become boastful, challenging one another, envying one another. [2]

Matthew Henry has an excellent comment on the fruit. He wrote:

> We must be fruitful. From a vine we look for grapes (Isaiah 5:2), and from a Christian, we look for Christianity; this is the fruit, a Christian temper and disposition, a Christian life and conversation, Christian devotions and Christian designs. We must honor God, and do good, and exemplify the purity and power of the religion we profess; and this is bearing fruit. The disciples here must be fruitful, as Christians, in all the fruits of righteousness, and as apostles, in diffusing the savor of the knowledge of Christ. [3]

To some degree, don't humans possess most if not all the virtues Paul enumerates in his letter to the Galatians? What is different about the Spirit's fruit? Just this: the Spirit's fruit is all about virtues that honor God; humans

---

[1] John 15:5
[2] Galatians 5:22-26
[3] Matthew Henry Bible Commentary (John 15). Retrieved from http://www. christianity.com/bible/commentary.php?com=mh&b=43&c=15

possess that which looks like virtues but are in reality not virtues at all since they have self at the core. Their tune, sung loudly or whispered softly, is always, "I, me, mine!"

So-called human virtues are in reality habits that are developing as soon as a child is old enough to talk and the parents are able to teach the child to hold back on the selfish core. Some people may be altruistic, philanthropic, and even exceptionally generous with their money, but a closer view will most likely reveal their core values are still self-centered; they need some return on their investment. The fruit of the Spirit is God-centered and other-centered; the spiritual person gives without thought of return or reward.

The fruit of the Spirit assists the believer in fulfilling the first and second commandments that Jesus articulated when asked which was the greatest commandment.

> Jesus answered, "The foremost is, 'Hear, O Israel! The Lord our God is one Lord; and you shall love the Lord your God with all your heart, and with all your soul, and with all your mind, and with all your strength.' The second is this, 'You shall love your neighbor as yourself.' There is no other commandment greater than these.[4]"

David Brown has written an exquisite paragraph on this passage of Scripture:

> It is as if He [Jesus] had said, "This is all Scripture in a nutshell; the whole law of human duty in a portable, pocket form." Indeed, it is so simple that a child may understand it, so brief that all may remember it, so comprehensive as to embrace all possible cases. And from its very nature it is unchangeable. It is inconceivable that God should require from his rational creatures anything less, or in substance anything else, under any dispensation, in any world, at any period throughout eternal duration. He cannot but claim this—all this—alike in heaven, in earth, and in hell! And this incomparable summary of the divine law belonged to the Jewish religion! As it shines in its own self-evidencing splendor, so it reveals its own true source. The religion from

---

[4] Mark 12:29-31, Deuteronomy 6:4

which the world has received it could be none other than a God-given religion! [5]

That said, the question inevitably and appropriately raised relative to both gifts and fruit is the simple question, "How?"

As to gifts, we discovered in the last lesson that when the disciples were filled (*plétho*) with the Holy Spirit, He distributed as He saw fit. Believers are to desire the best gifts, meaning gifts that will benefit their assembly's ministry or the ministry of an individual sent forth by the assembly.

As to fruit, we will discover in this lesson there is a different kind of filling that puts the believer on track for character renewal and personality changes, and all for the better! This is the path to maturing in the faith. The Scripture calls this "the renewing of the Holy Spirit."[6] Didn't we discuss 'filling' in the last chapter? Yes, we did, but this is a different role the Holy Spirit plays in the life of a believer. This is a different kind of filling.

II

The text to consider in this lesson is Ephesians 5:18. This text also uses the phrase, filled with the Spirit, but there is a difference between filled with the Spirit in Acts 2:4 and filled with the Spirit in Ephesians 5:18. The English translations don't show the difference because they use the same verb for both texts, and the verb used is 'filled.' Paul, however, uses a different Greek word for 'filled' in each verse. It is also a different verb tense. Both are significant.

In Ephesians 5:18, Paul uses the same Greek word that Luke uses in Acts 2:2 where Luke writes about the house "filled" with sound like that of a rushing wind. In the Ephesians text, Paul is not emphasizing the idea of control (fill = *plétho*) but emptiness (fill = *pléroö*). Paul uses the present imperative tense for the main verbs, "be not drunk" and "be filled." He also uses the present tense for all the participles that follow (i.e., the "–ing" words are the participles). The present tense indicates repeated or habitual action.

No doubt the translators preferred not to clutter the text so simply used 'filled' in both cases leaving the nuance to pastor-teachers.

---

[5] Brown, D. *The Gospel according to Mark (12:31): a Commentary*. In Jamieson, Fausset, and Brown Commentary.

[6] Romans 12:2 and 1 Titus 3:5

The New International Version (NIV) changes some of the Greek participles to imperatives but Greek grammarians frown on changing participles to imperatives. I quote from a volume on Greek grammar:

> Occasionally, though rarely, participles can function as though they were finite verbs and are not dependent on any verb in the context for their mood. The participle as an imperative is a case in point; this use of the participle is not attached to any verb in the context. But [A. T. Robertson says]: "in general it may be said that no participle should be explained this way that can properly be connected with a finite verb."[7]

In the *New Testament Greek Syntax,* we find similar comments relating to the imperative use of the participle:

> Imperatival participle. It must be independent of the main verb to be an imperatival participle. *Rare.*[8]

In the verses following verse 18, the participle phrases are *not* independent of the main verb. The participles, the –ing words, are very much dependent on the main verb theologically! And that main verb is 'filled.' The sense of the passage is this:

> Do not continue to be filled up with wine that has no redeeming value, but continue to be filled up with the Spirit; the redeeming value is that you will be able to be speaking to one another in psalms, hymns, and spiritual songs, singing and giving thanks always for everything in the name of our the Lord Jesus Christ to God the Father, making music from your heart to the Lord, and submitting to one another in reverence to Christ (especially wives to their own husbands).

Here is the Holman translation of the Ephesians passage and the verses that immediately follow.[9] See the box below; the participles are in bold print.

---

[7] The Berean Christian Bible Resources, grammar is a compilation primarily from Wallace and Mounce, Greek Grammar and Syntax, Greek Infinitive and Participle, *Edition: Feb. 10, 2009.* Retrieved from *http://www.bcbsr.com/greek/gvbls.html*

[8] Imperatival participle. *New Testament Greek Syntax.* Retrieved from http://www.lectionarystudies.com/syntax/syntaxpart.html

[9] Ephesians 5:18-22, Holman Christian Standard Bible (HCSB)

> And don't get drunk with wine,
> which leads to reckless actions,
> but be filled by the Spirit:
> **speaking** to one another in psalms,
> hymns, and spiritual songs,
> singing and making music
> from your heart to the Lord,
> **giving thanks** always for everything
> to God the Father
> in the name of our Lord Jesus Christ,
> **submitting** to one another in the fear
> of Christ, wives, submit [**submitting**] to
> your own husbands as to the Lord.

In verse 28, getting drunk leads to negative behavior; being filled with the Spirit leads to behavior beneficial to the entire assembly, as verses 19-22 indicate.

Presumably, the translators chose the imperatives to create several short sentences in place of Paul's long sentence. But that leads to a theological error: imperatives shift the responsibility to the individual rather than relying on the Holy Spirit to accomplish the ministries listed in the participles as Paul intended. Imperatives are saying all these ministries depend on "you" when in fact the Greek text is telling us they depend on being filled with the Holy Spirit.

Wallace comments on these verses,[10] calling these participles 'result participles.' They are the result of being filled with the Spirit. He says:

> Result participles are invariably present [tense] participles that follow the main verb; the idea of result here would suggest that the way in which one measures his/her success in fulfilling the command of [Ephesians] 5:18 is by the participles that follow (notice the progressive difficulty: from speaking God's word to being thankful for all, to being submissive to one another; such progression would, of course,

---

[10] Wallace. Daniel B. *The Participle.* Retrieved from http://www.Bible.org

immediately suggest that this filling is not instantaneous and absolute but progressive and relative.

The word 'submit' was probably inserted in verse 22 for linguistic reasons; it is not found in early manuscripts. Again, the insertion clouds the flow from the original word in verse 18. The grammar concerning a wife's relationship to her husband indicates that one looks back to the participle *'submitting'* found in verse 21 and that in turn looks back to *'filled'* in verse 18. Submitting willingly and graciously, one to another and especially wife to her husband, is not possible without a change in one's nature from the old to the new. That is possible only after one is filled with the Holy Spirit.

The Greek for the word *'filled'* is *pléroö* in verse 18 as already noted, meaning "to fill what is empty, fill up." It's like the expression we used to say to a gas station attendant, "Fill'r up, please." But the tank must be empty or part empty to be filled. This is part of the definition given in the Greek lexicon for *pléroö*: "to fill to the top: so that nothing shall be wanting, to full measure, fill to the brim." Something may already be there but it is not full.

When believers are born again, they are baptized in the Spirit, following which they may be filled *(plétho)* and manifest one of the gifts of the Spirit or they may be filled *(pléroö)* and have greater victory over some stubborn habit.

Being filled with the Holy Spirit starts when believers invite the Holy Spirit into the mind as per Romans 12:1-2. He enters the mind and begins housecleaning. Each sin He finds and brings to light must be acknowledged and confessed. The Greek word for 'confession' is literally "to agree with another." Confession is therefore agreeing with God that a value one holds or a behavior in which one engages is sinful.

When confession occurs, God forgives the sin—to remember it no more forever[11]—and the Holy Spirit fills the mind emptied of that sin with His presence. This enables the forgiven sinner to have a degree of mastery over that sin. Repeated confession of a sin is like digging up a dandelion—it is removed by degrees. Some sins are deep habits. For example, if the sin is impatience, acknowledgement, confession and the Father's forgiveness empties the mind of that sin and allows the Spirit to fill up that place in the mind now vacated with divine patience.

The verb tense Paul uses for *pléroö* in Ephesians 5:18 is present tense and in Greek the present tense conveys the idea of continued or habitual action. Being filled with the Spirit is an ongoing process. It can be translated,

[11] Hebrew 10:16-17

151

continue to be filled with the Spirit or filled continually. The Christian learns godly patience a little at a time, and the same is true of all the items found in the list of the fruit of the Spirit. As a dandelion with its entrenched roots, the Spirit recognizes the problem and is patient with believers as they struggle to uproot bad habits and bad behavior.

As noted previously, Luke does not use the emotion "joy" with *plétho* as we might expect because he does not see joy as an emotion that controls; it is not a mood of ecstasy. "Filled with joy" is not on that list. Rather Luke uses *pléroö* for this expression; see Acts 13:52, "And the disciples were filled with joy, and with the Holy Spirit." "Fill" in this text is in the perfect tense, indicating the continuation and present state of a completed past action.

Recap of Verbs

Acts 1:5 – baptized in the Holy Spirit

This is the Father's promise relayed to the disciples by Jesus, that the Holy Spirit will "come upon" them and at that time, they will receive power from on high; they will then become effective witnesses of the risen Christ in Jerusalem, Judea and Samaria, and to the ends of the earth. Did Jesus expect His disciples to be the ones who would take the Gospel to the ends of the earth? Probably not. But He did expect their children, their children's children, and et cetera to work until the job was done.

Baptism in the Holy Spirit and filled with the Holy Spirit were proof of their intimate relationship with Christ. This was firmly established by the gifts they manifested and also by their changed lives. As a result of being baptized (immersed) in the Holy Spirit, the disciples are called saints (holy people).[12] And, like the cucumber dipped in vinegar, they are permanently changed forever! The pickle is an end product and it cannot make any claim to beauty but as for the Christian, however, it is just a beginning. The Holy Spirit will continue to renew the mind and make the end product—the Christian— more and more beautiful. Jesus will then present the Church blameless and spotless to His Father as the Son's long awaited Bride.

As believers mature in the Faith, one day, the Holy Spirit will grant believers the privilege of standing perfect (complete) before the Father.

Acts 2:4 – filled (*plétho*) with the Spirit, aorist tense

---

[12] See 1 Corinthians 1:2

This is followed by a gift that the Spirit gives as needed for ministry; the gift on the day of Pentecost was speaking in tongues (foreign languages). Later, the Spirit filled the disciples with boldness, filled Stephen and gave him the privilege of seeing Jesus seated at the right hand of the Father, and filled the disciples so they could cast out demons.

Acts 2:2 and Ephesians 5:18, respectively – filled (*pléroö*) the house and filled (*pléroö*) with the Spirit

> ➤ In Acts 2:2, *pléroö* filled is aorist tense and refers to the sound that filled the house and then was gone.
> ➤ In Ephesians 5:18, *pléroö* filled is present tense and refers to repeated fillings. This is an ongoing renewal of the mind and the process of producing godly behavior, permitting believers to become blameless—one step at a time. [13]

---

[13] Additional example: Luke uses *pléroö* at Luke 2:40 where he speaks of Jesus as a child filled with wisdom; it is a participle, present tense; read: "continuously being filled with wisdom as He grew". He was learning concepts quickly and learning how to apply them wisely and appropriately.

Now to Him who is able to keep you

from stumbling,

and to make you stand

in the presence of His glory

blameless with great joy,

to the only God our Savior,

Jesus Christ our Lord,

be glory, majesty,

dominion and authority,

before all time and now and forever.

Amen.

CHAPTER 12

ASSURANCE OF SALVATION

Security of the Believer

I

Toward the end of his life, the Apostle Paul who proclaimed a message of freedom and peace and suffered much for it, wrote these words to Timothy, "his son in the faith":

For this reason I also suffer these things, but I am not ashamed; for I know whom I have believed and I am convinced that He is able to guard what I have entrusted to Him until that day. [1]

"Know...convinced...?" How could Paul be so sure? When he wrote these words to Timothy, he was a prisoner in Rome because of his faith in Jesus Christ. The threat of imminent death at the hands of an unpredictable Caesar did not deter him from his firm stand for Christ. His faith was well founded. But how did he experience such a feeling of security? Nowhere does he write, "once saved, always saved," but he is persuaded nevertheless that he is secure in Christ.

After several years of perfect attendance in Sunday School during my pre-teen years, I reached my teens and discovered I was the only one in the church who carried a Bible. The church was a good size and I loved the pipe organ, but I changed churches and began attending the church my parents

---

[1] 2 Timothy 1:12

were then attending. Not having an automobile, my parents were invited by some kind persons to go to their church. They offered to pick them up, a kind act that lasted for many years. People carried Bibles in that church and the pastor preached from the Bible every Sunday.

At a summer youth conference for teens, I affirmed my desire to follow Christ and that I would become a preacher someday. I had made the initial decision while I was very young.

I sympathize with those who have nagging doubts about their salvation because I had no assurance of my salvation. I needed someone to help me apply the biblical truths I was hearing and to encourage me in my walk with Christ. My parents were too busy running a corner grocery store (open from six a.m. to eleven p.m. seven days a week). They were aware of my decision to follow Christ and become a preacher and didn't think they had much to worry about because both of their children were looking forward to entering Bible school. But there were those nagging doubts. Was I saved or not saved?

On one occasion, my father urged me to go to the altar when an appeal was made for sinners to come forward. He thought that would be good for me and good for the church. Despite his urging, I resisted the invitations to go to the altar because I felt that they didn't apply to me. Frankly, I knew that I loved the Lord. But, in my father's day, everyone needed an altar experience. I recall hearing a member of the Builder generation crying out in frustration when he viewed the construction of a sister church that had no altar rail. He said, but "I was saved at an altar".

On another occasion, I was sitting in the balcony at a Jack Wyrtzen rally in New York City and when the appeal was made for those who wanted to get things right with the Lord to come forward, I felt uncomfortable. I had gotten things right with the Lord and "going forward" was not what I needed. I didn't know what I needed at the time but looking back on that time in my life, it is now clear to me that I needed mentoring to help me with the issue of assurance.

A young lady came to our congregation from another town. She had a Lutheran background where she had come to know the Lord. She was puzzled by the question, "When did you go to the altar?" Like me she didn't go to any altar, and like me, she was troubled by the question.

Tying one's religious experience to a place can be helpful but it is not the perfect solution for assurance. What if the church burns down and the altar rail is destroyed? In fact, several years after the older gentleman's remark about his appreciation for his altar experience, his church building burned to the ground. The grand piano, the Allen organ, the pulpit, the choir loft, and the altar rail, all destroyed!

In the last several decades of the twentieth century, many went forward to an altar and were saved in citywide rallies, but few were mentored. Statistics of those who went forward were carefully tabulated. To my knowledge, there wasn't any accounting for those who fell by the wayside. Although attrition was apparent, it was not the fault—or the responsibility—of the evangelist who moved on to another city or another summer camp. The responsibility lay at the feet of church members who, sadly, were not inclined to take new believers under their wing for mentoring.

Despite a lack of mentoring, I persevered and became a pastor and an international worker. In addition, I found a wonderful woman to marry and together we dedicated our lives to serving others.

II

I was on a 14-hour flight to Amman, Jordan. It was a large plane filled with passengers including a large church group from West Virginia. The plane hit heavy rain just before landing and was struck by lightning. The plane shuddered and the lights went out. A few moments later, a backup system put the lights back on and one of the West Virginian group shouted (appropriately) "Hallelujah!" We landed safely at Amman's small airport.

The West Virginia group was exuberant about their faith and occasionally during the flight buttonholed someone walking down the aisle to ask if they were saved. One of the group said to me pointblank, "Hello, are you saved?" I answered in the affirmative. "Then you speak in tongues," was the follow up. It was a declarative sentence with much conviction but the look on the young lady's face told me she was waiting for a response. "No, I don't speak in tongues." I walked on to the lavatory.

Later in the flight, another member of the group asked me the same question with the same follow up comment about tongues. The assurance of their salvation was speaking in "tongues." Their reference to tongues was not a reference to foreign languages, but what they called a heavenly language, the language of angels, or a "spiritual tongue."

Do I have a gift from the Holy Spirit? Yes, but it is not tongues; it is the blessed experience of being called as a pastor-teacher. (See Chapter 10: Filled with the Spirit - *Gifts*.) Can't their tongues be a proof of having the Holy Spirit and thus providing them with the assurance of their salvation? Yes, indeed. However, when they implied that I wasn't fully saved if I didn't speak in tongues, they were not taught accurately. If they were depending on speaking in tongues for their assurance of salvation, they will find their faith attacked by the evil one and their faith at that time will prove to be very wobbly!

When fully engaged in serving the Lord, there is occasionally a need for a gift from the Holy Spirit to affirm the Word being shared. He will bless the servant of the Lord with exactly what he or she needs at the time. It could be tongues[2] or it could be one of the many other gifts mentioned in the chapter on gifts. He will distribute what is needed as He sees fit, as noted previously. It quite conceivably may be a word of wisdom or knowledge.

Every Christian wants to feel assured of and be secure in his or her relationship with Jesus Christ. Who doesn't want to feel as assured as the Apostle Paul?

Meditating on Hebrews 11 will bring a great deal of peace in the matter of assurance. There's a long list of individuals who believed they heard God speaking, obeyed, and saw much blessing. These are "heroes of the faith" who pleased God. Before discussing faith and its importance, there is another issue to understand and it is found in the second part of Hebrews 11:6:

> … for he who comes to God must believe that He is and that
> He is a rewarder of those who seek Him.

If you cannot believe there is a God in Heaven because you cannot prove He is there, try this: pray to Him sincerely as though He was there—talk to Him as you would to a friend—and you will find He will answer you. You can start this way, "God, if you are there, please…" If you say, "So I'll pray for a Mercedes-Benz automobile. Will He answer that prayer?" No, He will not. He answers prayers that advance His kingdom and bless His servants who want to see His kingdom advanced.

There is no room for atheists here or for doubting Thomases. To believe He exists requires faith; that's what the word "believe" means. However, to believe there is a God means the individual must quit playing God. Incidentally, there are few true atheists; many who are have a god and it is the almighty "I".

Barnes offers the following comment on this passage in Hebrews:

---

[2] The gift of tongues was a sign gift for unbelievers. See 1 Corinthians 14:22.

The declaration here implies more than that there should be a general persuasion of the truth that there is a God. It is necessary that we have this belief... in the act of drawing near to him, and that we should realize that we are actually in the presence of the all-seeing Jehovah.[3]

James explains that demons 'believe' and the Christian must have more than that kind of faith. He wrote, "You believe that God is one. You do well; the demons also believe, and shudder."[4] The "burning question" is this: "How do I know the voice I hear in my head is the Lord's and not just a figment of my own imagination?" It's the Lord's if it is confirmed by a principle in the Bible, by godly people who also pray diligently, and by circumstances that begin to fall into place. Be careful: do not look to circumstances first, do not search until somebody agrees with you, and finally do not look for a biblical principle that (tweaked) seems to fit your desire. That is backwards. That voice in your head is not the Lord's.

The following order shows the faith that pleases God and how it differs from that of demons:

1. Be willing to believe there is a God (many resist like the demons because of not wanting to lose control—it's a power thing).

2. Believe that God loves you and is desirous of establishing a relationship with you (quit playing God; Satan found himself kicked out of heaven for doing just that[5]—it's an ego thing).

3. Believe that God rewards those who seek Him (He has sensibilities like a person; many assume they know better than God).

There are some folk, mostly men I venture to say, who are so rationally minded they believe everything must have proof. Yes, there are proofs that God exists. First, no other religion has a God that has revealed Himself as a God of holiness and purity, and a God who expects His people, Jews and Christians alike, to lead holy and pure lives. Second, since human beings cannot do that on their own, He has given His Holy Spirit to believers who love His Son, Jesus Christ, to help them do just that.

---

[3] Barnes Notes, Hebrews 11:1
[4] James 2:19
[5] Isaiah 14:12f, Ezekiel 28

A woman of retirement age led a painful life. I'll call her Judith. Her family did painful things to her. She was sent to live in another country to escape pending war but shortly after arriving there, war broke out in the country where she went to live. She married and had an unhappy marriage; and she had a family who grew up in American boomer culture that she didn't understand. What did this lady need? She needed love! Some Christians saw the need and showered her with kindness. That's what every Christian should be doing.

One day, this lady said, "I have never known anyone as kind as my (Christian) neighbors!" Mature Christians are overjoyed at being kind, even though practicing kindness is not natural to any human being. It is God's gift to His servants. Her statement affirmed the faith of these Christians!

We can feel badly, however, when we know there are other Christians who do not understand that their neighbors are hurting and need love. Obedience to God and expressing kindness is the way neighbor dynamics should work.

Now we return to Hebrews 11 and discuss the issue of faith.

Faith

The declaration in the Book of Hebrews tells us, "Without faith it is impossible to please God."[6] Since there is a double negative in that statement, the positive statement would read: "With faith it is possible to please God." Hebrews 11 is a roll call of men and women who by their faith pleased God.

In Hebrews 11, all the individuals listed are presented as examples of faith. Abraham is seen as the father of those who take God at His Word. Faith is believing in something even though you cannot at first prove its reality. We see nothing when we engage a light switch, but we believe the lights will illuminate. And they do! When remote controls first appeared on the scene, we tentatively pushed a button and voilà! the automobile door unlocked, the garage door opened, or the television changed channels! We said, "Wow!" And we have enjoyed the devices ever since.

> Now faith is the assurance of things hoped for, the conviction of things not seen.[7]

How did Abraham get that far along in his faith? How did he learn to take God at His word? Scripture does not say. Abraham was monotheistic in

---

[6] Hebrews 11:6
[7] Hebrews 11:1

an idolatrous world; his father, Terah, was an idolater.[8] Abraham took what he believed he was hearing from God as 'gospel truth,' as bizarre as the word from the Lord seemed at the moment. He communicated with the God of Heaven and pleased God because of his faith. Although old and childless, this is the promise God covenanted with him:

> As for Me, behold, My covenant is with you,
> And you will be the father of a multitude of nations.[9]

God also said he would become as many as the stars in the heavens.[10] Both prophecies have been fulfilled.

The Apostle Paul devotes the fourth chapter of his letter to the Romans to the faith of Abraham, emphasizing the fact that Abraham did not please God because of what he did but because he took God at his word. Here is the critical verse: Abraham was "fully assured that what God had promised, He was able also to perform."[11]

One day, God asked Abraham to take his son Isaac to Mt. Moriah and offer him there as a sacrifice. Despite the fact that Isaac was the son that God promised to him and his wife Sarah in their old age, Abraham believed this was God speaking to him, so he obeyed. Abraham's obedience demonstrated that he loved God most of all. Because of this, as Abraham was ready to plunge the knife into his son, God stopped him and instructed him to sacrifice a ram caught in a thicket nearby.[12]

What was his faith based on? We are not told the details but we do know God led him step by step and that's how faith builds up for a big test that will come when He thinks we are ready.

As to assurance, Charles Haddon Spurgeon says, "We do not have to go through life without the assurance of salvation." In 1 John 5:13 the apostle John says, "These things have I written unto you...that you may know that you have eternal life." How do we know? Basically, by the word of God!

However, Abraham's first message may have been the heavens. Maybe one in a million or one in a billion gets the message from the heavens. But the message is there for anyone who will take time to 'read' it. Here's the word from the heavens:

---

[8] Joshua 24:2
[9] Genesis 17:4
[10] Genesis 15:5
[11] Romans 4:21
[12] cf. Genesis 22:13

The heavens declare the glory of God; the skies proclaim the
work of his hands.[13]

If you have faith, it will be tested. Abraham's faith was. What was the
purpose of this? I assure you, obeying God is more important than any
possession believers have, including a cherished, only child. It was not a
charade. Here's the key verse:

[God] said, "Do, not stretch out your hand against the lad,
and do nothing to him; for now I know that you fear God,
since you have not withheld your son, your only son from
Me."[14]

How difficult that was for Abraham! If you follow God, you don't know
what he will require of you but like Abraham, he will require you to offer
Him your most treasured possession. As a Christian you may protest and say,
"I've never heard God talk to me like he talked to Abraham!" or "God liked
Abraham better than He likes me." Sorry, that would be favoritism and God
doesn't play favorites.

Neither vision nor mission statement can be effective without faith! In
a booklet entitled *George Mueller, Man of Faith*,[15] George Mueller himself
describes faith. He wrote:

What is faith? In the simplest manner in which I am able
to express it, I answer: Faith is the assurance that the thing
which God has said in His Word is true, and that God
will act according to what He has said in His Word. This
assurance, this reliance on God's Word, this confidence is
faith.

Viewing the matter negatively, we may say that faith is not a
matter of impressions, or of probabilities, or of appearances.
Impressions come from human reasoning, which at best is
untrustworthy. Faith on the other hand is based upon the
impregnable Word of God. It is not impression, strong or
weak, that will make any difference...

---

[13] Psalms 19:1
[14] Genesis 22:12
[15] Zondervan Books, publisher

...There is so much dependence upon impressions, probabilities, appearances, and similar unimportant issues that we have so little blessing among us. All these things must be abandoned. The naked Word of God is what we are to depend upon. That is enough for us.

We run helter-skelter and then go into our place of prayer. Willy-nilly, we throw a bunch of requests at the Lord. We take a deep breath and wait—and even threaten to hold it until He answers. Then we grow impatient, irritable, resentful and just plain angry because He seems to answer others' prayers but not our own. Let me quote again from George Mueller's story because his faith reveals a strong kinship to Abraham.

"The children are dressed and ready for school. But there is no food for them to eat," the housemother of the orphanage informed George Mueller. George asked her to take the 300 children into the dining room and have them sit at the tables. He thanked God for the food and waited. George knew God would provide food for the children as he always did. Within minutes, a baker knocked on the door. "Mr. Mueller," he said, "last night I could not sleep. Somehow I knew that you would need bread this morning. I got up and baked three batches for you. I will bring it in."

Soon, there was another knock at the door. It was the milkman. His cart had broken down in front of the orphanage. The milk would spoil by the time the wheel was fixed. He asked George if he could use some free milk. George smiled as the milkman brought in ten large cans of milk. It was just enough for the 300 thirsty children.[16]

Did you catch the key phrase? Here it is again: "George knew God would provide." That begs the question, "How did George know?"

How did Abraham know God wanted him to leave his kinfolk in Ur of the Chaldees and travel to a new place and live there?

How did Moses know he was to return to Egypt and lead the Israelites to the Promised Land?

We are given some details about Moses' calling. He saw a burning bush as he was tending sheep and went to look it because it burned but was not

---

[16] Christianity.com, George Mueller, Orphanages Built by Prayer

consumed. It was God's doing. Close to the bush he heard God's voice commissioning him to return to Egypt and bring the Israelites out of Egypt. When he protested, the Lord said He already had called Moses' brother Aaron to come and get Moses and to be Moses' spokesperson.

God speaks in a variety of ways and the Christian must be willing to listen. When he or she truly hears from God the result is overwhelming peace.

The Seeker Must Be Righteous

There is yet another dimension to assurance; it is the issue of righteousness. The Word tells us Christ is made to us righteousness, so always keep that in mind:

> But by [God's] doing you are in Christ Jesus, who became to
> us wisdom from God, and righteousness and sanctification,
> and redemption.[17]

Speaking of righteousness, scripture singles out the following individuals as people who heard from God. What they had in common was that they were all spoken of as 'righteous.' The list includes Noah,[18] Zechariah and Elizabeth (John the Baptist's parents)[19], Mary and Joseph[20], Joseph of Arimathea,[21] Cornelius,[22] and Lot.[23] They wanted to hear from God but while waiting, they continued to please God. David says of the righteous:

> For it is You who blesses the righteous man, O Lord,
>
> You surround him with favor as with a shield.[24]

If one is to hear from God a prerequisite is righteousness. How do we become righteous? Another lesson from Abraham's life says, "Then he believed in the Lord; and He reckoned it to him as righteousness."[25] That word "reckoned" can also mean 'imputed' and the sense is "calculated to Abraham's account."

---

[17] 1 Corinthians 1:20
[18] Genesis 6:9
[19] Luke 1:5
[20] Matthew 1:18
[21] Luke 23:50
[22] Acts 10:22
[23] 2 Peter 2:7-9
[24] Psalm 5:12 (see also Psalm 7)
[25] Genesis 15:6

The Christian's God is sovereign. The person secure in Christ knows he or she has a God who knows what He is doing and will do what is best for His children. A very comforting thought is found in Romans 8:28 and this verse is worth framing:

> We know that God causes all things
> to work together for good to those who love God,
> to those who are called according to His purpose.

No one tells God what to do or advises Him in what He has purposed. Satan tries to block Him at every turn, and human beings reveling in self-will, ignore Him. But God will not be blocked nor will He be ignored! The Christian's God is sovereign over nations and kings. [26] Unlike the gods of the Greeks, our God is not capricious. He is always ready to talk to those who love Him. When He talks to you, you will know it!

The San Diego Christian College has posted the following online, answering the question of assurance:

> We should find the assurance of our salvation in the objective truth of God's Word.
>
> We should have confident trust that we are saved based on the promises God has declared, not because of our subjective experiences. [27]

Let the Apostle Paul's words to Timothy encourage you. Paul was suffering, but his words have a resounding ring of confidence in the God he was serving. His statement is not fatalistic, but rather so positive that it should give you goose bumps—it surely does me!

---

[26] Psalm 47:7-8, Daniel 2:37
[27] San Diego Christian College web site: http://www.gotquestions.org

James M. Riccitelli

> For this reason I also suffer these things,
> but I am not ashamed; for I know whom
> I have believed and
> I am convinced that He is able
> to guard what I have entrusted to Him
> until that day.[203]

---

[28] Second Timothy 1:12

HOW AUTHENTIC IS YOUR FAITH?

I

Now that you have read through this book, did you find out how much you know and more importantly, how much you did not know? There are significant dangers to a lack of knowledge, especially biblical knowledge. The purpose of this book is to dispel biblical illiteracy and strengthen Christians in their faith.

Let me spell out five dangers of biblical illiteracy: first, one is no longer aware of the Heavenly Father's wishes; second, one will risk displeasing the Father; third, one's fellowship with the Father is broken; fourth, one's heart is filled with unrest; and fifth, one's prayers will not be heard by the Father, as the book of Proverbs states:

> Then they will call on me, but I will not answer; they will seek me diligently but they will not find me, because they hated knowledge and did not choose the fear of the LORD.[1]

A break in intimacy with the Father is subtle but, upon reflection, a believer usually knows when a break occurs because there is guilt and shame. Adam and Eve knew. And what did they do? Their next move was to hide themselves in the beautiful garden God had made for their pleasure.

Adam and Eve were created to bear the imprint of the Heavenly Father. He created them "in His own *tselem, tselem,*" that is, "in His own image, image." So Genesis 2 reads. Don't miss the repeated word used for emphasis.

---

[1] Proverbs 1:28

This word, *tselem,* means, "image, likeness, or resemblance" according to the Hebrew lexicon. In addition, the Genesis account tells us that God "breathed into his nostrils the breath of life; and man became a living being." Remember that the Hebrew word for 'breath' also means 'spirit,' so God breathed His breath/Spirit into Adam.

What does all this mean? Like God, humans are spiritual, rational, and emotional beings. And like God, humans are moral beings with the ability to choose what is right or wrong.

What do you suppose God expected from Adam and Eve? Having a will to choose, did they choose what was right and pleasing to the Father or did they disobey and choose what was pleasing to them? You know the story— they chose the latter. Notice the emotion packed into this critical event:

> When the woman saw that the tree was good for food,
> and that it was a delight to the eyes, and that the tree was
> desirable to make one wise, she took from its fruit and ate;
> and she gave also to her husband with her, and he ate.[2]

Satan confused Eve about the beautiful gift God gave her (her emotions). The New Testament, referring to this event, says Eve was deceived.[3] Adam on the other hand, took and ate with his eyes wide open; he made a conscious decision to disobey. So the New Testament says of Adam, "As in Adam, all die."[4] His test was a test for the human race. He failed and passed his 'fallen nature' on to his children, his children's children, and all who followed. Everyone is born with a sinful nature. How long does a child take to learn the word, "No"?

What did God expect of Adam? Obedience! And that is exactly what He expects from every believer. When one is obedient to God, the values imbedded in one's mind are sanctified by the faithful work of the Holy Spirit—one by one. They are set apart from sin for God's glory.

Remember this: If you are a Christian, God *declares* you to be holy. With the various tests He allows you to go through, you *become* sanctified (holy) to the degree that you are obedient. This is the path to Christlikeness. The fruit of the Spirit will become more and more evident in your life. Others will note that you are becoming more loving, more joyful, more peaceful, more

---

[2] Genesis 3:6
[3] 1 Timothy 2:14
[4] 1 Corinthians 15:22

patient, more kind, good and faithful, and more gentle and self-controlled (Galatians 5:22-23).

Did you ever tie a string around your finger to help you remember something you needed to do? Your string might have been to remind you to stop and pick up your dry cleaning on the way home after work. God, always ready to encourage His people to live a holy life, didn't direct the Israelites to tie a string around their finger but instead to use tassels. Here's the text where we see tassels were to be used for the purpose of reminding them of two critical matters—do all Yahweh's commandments and be holy:

> Speak to the sons of Israel, and tell them that they shall make for themselves tassels on the corners of their garments throughout their generations, and that they shall put on the tassel of each corner a cord of blue. It shall be a tassel for you to look at and remember all the commandments of the LORD, so as to do them and not follow after your own heart and your own eyes, after which you played the harlot, so that you may remember to do all My commandments and be holy to your God.[5]

Yes, contemporary Christians need to be reminded as well. That's the beauty of Christian fellowship: one can encourage another to live a holy life. Christianity doesn't suggest using tassels or pieces of string, but rather laying one's Bible in a conspicuous place so that it will serve as a reminder to open it often. Yes, the Bible can serve as a tassel for the Christian.

And don't forget to offer God your sacrifices. Sacrifices? Contemporary Christians are not Old Testament saints offering lambs and oxen as sacrifices to the Lord. What sacrifice are we to offer? The Christian's Sacrifice has already been given once and for all, even Jesus, who was crucified as a sin offering. We are New Testament saints. What do we have to offer? First, we are to offer ourselves as a thank offering according to Romans 12:1, which says, "present yourself [as] a living sacrifice to God." Second, turning to the book of Hebrews, we find the writer exhorting new Jewish Christians:

> And do not neglect doing good and sharing, for with such sacrifices God is pleased.[6]

---

[5] Numbers 15:38-40
[6] Hebrews 13:16

When is it time to move on from milk to "meat and potatoes"? Answer: Whenever a Christian is grounded in the fundamentals of the Christian faith. Important is the exhortation also found in the book of Hebrews, "Forget not the assembling of yourselves together"[7] Make it a practice to hear a pastor-teacher expound the Word. That means, "Gather together for edification and scatter for evangelism."[8]

We covered the subject of holiness (sanctification) rather extensively in Chapter 6. It was important because it set Israel apart from every other nation on earth. The tassel-reminders were not trivial but an important part of Israel's culture. As the leadership backslid, look at what happened to the tassels. Jesus chided the religious hierarchy's hypocrisy of His day, saying:

> But they do all their deeds to be noticed by men; for they broaden their phylacteries[9] and lengthen the tassels of their garments.[10]

Obviously, the leadership needed to authenticate their faith and Jesus attempted to help them do it. But the leadership had a problem with accepting Jesus and they were not going to allow Him to instruct them. They concluded:

> Is not this the carpenter's son? Is not His mother called Mary, and His brothers, James and Joseph and Simon and Judas?[11]

II

Christians serve a unique God. He formulated the plan of salvation before He created the first man and woman. Why did He do that? We don't know all God's reasons but the Bible gives a hint or two.[12] However, we do know love had a great deal to do with it as John 3:16 tells us. Love needs an object and He created human beings to be the object of His affection. He foresaw

---

[7] Hebrews 10:25
[8] Halverson, late chaplain of the United States Senate
[9] Phylacteries are either of two small square leather boxes containing slips inscribed with scriptural passages and traditionally worn on the left arm and on the head by observant Jewish men and especially adherents of Orthodox Judaism during morning weekday prayers. Retrieved from http://www.merriam-webster.com
[10] Matthew 23:5
[11] Matthew 13:55
[12] See Isaiah 43:7, Revelation 4:11

the events in the Garden of Eden. He knew human beings would need to be redeemed, Satan's rule over this world terminated, and final judgment pronounced on him.

Here is a part of Jesus' prayer indicating that the love of God existed before Adam and Eve appeared on the scene.

> Father, I desire that they also, whom You have given Me, may see My glory which You have given Me, for You loved Me before the foundation of the world.[13]

To bring about man's salvation, God prepared for it well in advance. Today, God invites the world to be part of this glorious salvation: "Today if you hear his voice, do not harden your hearts."[14]

God played three roles to bring this plan of salvation to fruition, rescuing those He created from the clutches of Satan, the god of this world.[15] The roles are Father, Son, and Holy Spirit. Please appreciate God's willingness to adopt these roles; this was all part of His planning ahead "from the foundation of the world." And the plan covers "from everlasting to everlasting."[16]

The Apostle John notes how personal the plan of God is; it isn't just for the inanimate creation which is waiting to be set free from its "slavery to corruption,"[17] but rather for the world (again, see John 3:16). He desires to bring Jews and Gentiles into His family. In the following verse, note several things: whom He chooses, the grounds on which He chooses, when He chose, and what He chose believers for. This is a compelling reason why believers in Christ should authenticate their faith. Paul wrote:

(WHO?) Just as He chose us

(WHAT GROUNDS?) in Him [Christ]

(WHEN?) before the foundation of the world,

(WHY?) that we would be holy and blameless before Him.

(WHAT CONTEXT?) In love

(PURPOSE?) He predestined us to adoption as sons

---

13 John 17:25
14 Hebrews 4:7
15 2 Corinthians 4:4
16 Psalm 103:17
17 Romans 8:21, 22

(MEANS?) through Jesus Christ to Himself

(MOTIVATION?) according to the kind intention of His will[18]

Not one of Egypt's 2000 gods, nor any of the many gods of the Babylonians, the Greeks, or the Romans could bring a lasting peace or encourage a people to be holy, pure, and good. Nor can any of the gods of the twenty-first century American culture—and there are many! Only the God of Heaven, the God who created the heavens and the earth and all that is therein, could have prepared such a magnificent plan. And the Bible tells us clearly that He did!

The Old Testament and the New Testament are all about God's plan that was birthed in love and kindness, with hopes that unbelievers will know it, understand it, and embrace it. Believers everywhere will know who Jesus Christ really is and know the foundational truths about salvation outlined in this book. Every believer can live what they say they believe.

So, how authentic is your faith?

---

[18] Ephesians 1:4

Meditate on Peter's Words

Grace and peace be multiplied to you in the knowledge of God and of Jesus our Lord; seeing that His divine power has granted to us everything pertaining to life and godliness, through the true knowledge of Him who called us by His own glory and excellence. For by these He has granted to us His precious and magnificent promises, so that by them you may become partakers of the divine nature, having escaped the corruption that is in the world by lust.

Now for this very reason also, applying all diligence, in your faith supply moral excellence, and in your moral excellence, knowledge, and in your knowledge, self-control, and in your self-control, perseverance, and in your perseverance, godliness, and in your godliness, brotherly kindness, and in your brotherly kindness, love.

For if these qualities are yours and are increasing, they render you neither useless nor unfruitful in the true knowledge of our Lord Jesus Christ. For he who lacks these qualities is blind or shortsighted, having forgotten his purification from his former sins.

Therefore, brethren, be all the more diligent to make certain about His calling and choosing you; for as long as you practice these things, you will never stumble for in this way the entrance into the eternal kingdom of our Lord and Savior Jesus Christ will be abundantly supplied to you.

2 Peter 1:2-11

SELF-ASSESSMENT

✢✢✢✢✢

The assessment that follows is designed
to be reviewed after reading the entire book.

Authenticate Your Faith!

By testing your knowledge

If you cannot answer a question, refer back to
the appropriate chapter or scripture.
After finding the correct answer, delay filling in the blank until
you have learned the material.

Part 1: The unique difference between the Founder of the Christian faith, Jesus, and every other religious leader.

Chapter 1. Introducing the Man from Nazareth aka Podunk

    a. What is the meaning of Podunk?
    Answer:

    b. Why does the author use the term Podunk to describe Nazareth?
    Answer:

    c. Where was Jesus born?
    Answer:

    d. Why did Jesus grow up in Nazareth?
    Answer:

    e. The Messiah came from the house (lineage/stock) of whom?
    Answer:

    f. The Messiah came from which town?
    Answer:

g. Why was the leadership in Jerusalem so sure Jesus came from Galilee, a fact Jesus could never deny?
Answer:

h. This chapter shows the humanity of Jesus. Who was Jesus' mother?
Answer:

i. In Matthew 16:13, Jesus refers to Himself as the Son of whom?
Answer:

j. God used that same phrase in Matthew 16:13 and multiple times in the Old Testament for a prophet. Which prophet? [Hint: it begins with the letter E. One of the Old Testament books bears his name].
Answer:

k. Why can it be said that Jesus was fully a human being?
Answer:

l. What human feelings did Jesus experience?
Answer:

m. Hebrews 4:15 says Jesus was tempted "in all things" but without what?
Answer:

Chapter 2. Introducing the Man from Heaven *aka* His Father's House

a. Who referred to Heaven as His "Father's House"?
Answer:

b. Where in the Gospel of John is this reference found?
Answer:

c. As Jesus sat in the synagogue in Nazareth, who did He say He was?
Answer:

d. What Scripture did Jesus use to back His claim?
Answer:

e. This claim made the men in the synagogue angry. What did they try to do to Jesus?
Answer:

f. Jesus escaped and moved to a town located on the northern shore of the Lake of Galilee. What was this town called?
Answer:

g. At what age did Jesus start His ministry?
Answer:

h. Jesus was baptized in the Jordan River by whom?
Answer:

i. What promise did the one who baptized Jesus make? [Hint: One day he would baptize them with the…]
Answer:

j. What unique phenomenon occurred at Jesus' baptism?
Answer:

Chapter 2 *continued*

k. What was the biggest stumbling block for Jewish leadership?
Answer:

l. According to Jewish leaders, Jesus was committing blasphemy by making Himself equal with whom?
Answer:

m. Chapter 2 shows the deity of Jesus. Why is it imperative that Jesus was both fully human and also had God as His Father?
Answer:

n. Why did John record the works of Jesus according to John 20:31?
Answer:

Chapter 3. Salvation! Perfect Timing!
"The Fullness of Time"

a. There are many Old Testament prophecies concerning the first coming of the Messiah. What does Micah 5:2 tell us about the birthplace of the Messiah?
Answer:

b. In that same verse, Micah (c. 750 BC) also foretold a vital piece of information about the Messiah existence. This information was overlooked by the Jews when Mary and Joseph registered their newborn with the government for tax purposes. What specifically did Micah say about the Messiah's existence that the Jews missed?
Answer:

c. Why couldn't the Jews figure out *when* the Messiah would be born?
Answer:

d. What is the significance of Matthew 24:14?
Answer:

e. In what way does Matthew 28:19-20 complement Matthew 24:14?
Answer:

Summary:

What stands out for you in Chapters 1 to 3? What will help you in your walk with the Lord? Write your thoughts below.

Part 2: The meaning of salvation.

The Lord Jesus used the word 'saved' many times. In the New Testament according to the Blue Letter Bible.org, 'saved' appears 104 times in 104 verses in the King James version, and 89 times in 89 verses in the New American Standard Bible.

Chapter 4. Saved!
God's Comprehensive Plan

a. This chapter familiarizes you with the three terms that comprise salvation for a believer. What are they? [Hint: #1 is Past tense, #2 is present tense, and #3 is future tense]
Answers:

   #1: R
   #2: S
   #3: G

b. What other terms can be used for the past tense?
Answer:

c. Can all believers pinpoint a time when this occurs?
Answer:

e. What other term can be used for the present tense?
Answer:

f. Why can most believers pinpoint the commencement of this event? (Tie your answer in with Romans 12:10)
Answer:

g. When did God plan all this?
Answer:

Chapter 5. Saved From Sin!

Born Twice

a. What does it mean to be born twice?
   Answer:

b. What does 'regeneration' literally mean?
   Answer:

c. In this first phase of salvation, how is the believer saved from spiritual death? (See Romans 5:12)
   Answer:

d. Why do we need to be born again?
   Answer:

e. What is expected of us after we are born again? (See Ephesians 2:10).
   Answer:

Chapter 6. Saved From Self!
Growing Up Christian

a. What does it mean to be sanctified?
   Answer:

b. Observing those who claim to be Christian, what would you expect to see as you observe their lives?
   Answer:

c. In this second phase of salvation, the believer is saved from what?
   Answer:

d. What does I Corinthians 13 say about love? List any virtue that presents the most difficulty for you in your walk with the Lord.
   Answer:

e. What is the will of God for believers? (See I Thessalonians 4.)
   Answer:

f. What additional blessings does the believer have when s/he accepts Christ as Savior and Lord? (See I Corinthians 1:30).
   Answers:

   1.
   2.
   3.
   4.

Chapter 7. Saved From the Wrath of God!
The Diploma

    a.   What will we be saved from at the time of the third phase of salvation?
       Answer:

    b.   What happens to a believer who dies?
       Answer:

    c.   Christians believe in the resurrection of the dead. Explain.
       Answer:

    d.   Who will be glorified?
       Answer:

    e.   What will a glorified body be like?
       Answer:

    f.   When will believers be glorified?
       Answer:

Summary:

What stands out for you in Chapters 4 to 7? What will help you in your walk with the Lord? Write your thoughts below.

Part 3: Water Baptism

Chapter 8. First Step of Obedience

a. Why is water baptism called the first step of obedience?
Answer:

b. Who baptized Jesus?
Answer:

c. Why was Jesus baptized? Check Matthew 3 and Mark 1.
Answer:

d. Did Jesus command His disciples to baptize new believers? The answer is 'yes.' Where is that found in the Gospels?
Answer:

e. Who baptized the original twelve disciples?
Answer:

f. To what did Paul compare the dipping of candidates into the water?
Answer:

g. To what did Paul compare the coming up out of the water?
Answer:

h. A local church may require baptism if a believer requests membership. That's a local church's preference, but the source of that requirement is not found in the Bible, rather, it will be found in the church's what?
Answer:

Summary:

What stands out for you in Chapter 8? What will help you in your walk with the Lord? Write your thoughts below.

Part 4: The Holy Spirit in the Life of a Believer

Chapter 9: Baptized *in* the Holy Spirit
The Holy Spirit and the Believer (1)

a. What does the Greek word *baptizo* mean?
    Answer:

b. What is the meaning of the word baptism when used in relation to the Holy Spirit?
    Answer:

c. In Acts 1:5, Jesus draws a parallel between the Holy Spirit and the medium John used, that is, the Jordan (River). Why can we believe immersion was used?
    Answer:

d. The author cites three passages that are grammatically identical. In each passage, individuals or groups were said to be baptized as followers or disciples of a particular leader. They were also baptized in a particular medium. Identify the leader and the medium in which each individual was baptized.

    1 Corinthians 10:2 states that all were baptized (a) into whom and (b) with/in what medium?
    Answers:
    (a)   (b)

    Acts 19:3 states that all were baptized (a) into whom and (b) with/in what medium?
    Answers:
    (a)   (b)

    Galatians 3:27 states that all were baptized (a) into whom and (b) with/in what medium?
    Answers:
    (a)   (b)

Chapter 9 *continued*

   e.   How much water touched the Israelites when they crossed the Red Sea?

      Answer:

   f.   If baptize means *to immerse*, how does Paul justify using the word for the Israelites when they crossed the Red Sea?

      Answer:

Chapter 10: Filled with the Spirit: Gifts
The Holy Spirit and the Believer (2)

a. When were the disciple baptized in the Holy Spirit and how do we know this?
Answer:

b. On what day were the disciples baptized *with* the Holy Spirit?
Answer:

c. What was the first gift the Holy Spirit gave to the fledgling Church and why was this particular gift given?
Answer:

d. The Jewish leaders did not come to hear what the disciples had to say. What was unusual about the crowd that gathered?
Answer:

e. According to Acts 2, after hearing Peter's sermon, how many came to know Christ as Savior and Lord and were baptized?
Answer:

f. Acts reveals that the early church exercised more than one gift. Name these gifts:
Answer:

g. Very soon after Pentecost, the disciples prayed for another gift. What was that gift and did the Holy Spirit answer their prayer?
Answer:

Chapter 10 *continued*

h. According to Acts 1:8, there were four locations where new believers received the Holy Spirit and spoke in tongues. What were the locations and, according to Acts 2, 8, 10, and 19, who were the believers?

Answers:

See	The Locations	See	The Believers
Act 1:8	Jerusalem	Acts 2	Jews
Act 1:8		Acts 8	
Act 1:8		Acts 10	
Act 1:8		Acts 19	

Chapter 11 - Filled with the Spirit: Fruit
The Holy Spirit and the Believer (3)

a. Where does one go in the Bible to find the fruit of the Spirit?
    Answer:

b. List the nine fruit of the Spirit:
    Answer:

c. Human virtues honor what?
    Answer:

d. The virtues that are Holy Spirit empowered honor whom?
    Answer:

e. Believers are to desire earnestly the best gifts. What are the best gifts?
    Answer:

f. In 1 Corinthians 12:30, Paul says there is a more "excellent way." What is the more excellent way? To answer this question, remember that the chapter divisions are not in the original text but were added later for convenience. [Hint: The answer is a four-letter word]
    Answer:

g. Explain Ephesians 5:18.
    Answer:

h. What specific godly behaviors listed in Ephesians 5 result from this filling? (verses 19-22). [Hint: they are participles that end in "ing"]
    Answer:

Chapter 11 *continued*

i. These behaviors are dependent on the verb found in Ephesians 5:18 which is:
    Answer:

j. Is this filling given to confirm a particular ministry like the filling in Acts 2:4 or is it constant, lifelong experiences, that is, repeated fillings?
    Answer:

Summary:

What stands out for you in Chapters 9, 10, and 11? What will help you in your walk with the Lord? Write your thoughts below.

PART 6: The question of assurance

Chapter 12 - Assurance of Salvation: Security of the Believer

a. What is the best source that provides assurance of salvation?
Answer:

b. The believer appropriates the truth by exercising what?
Answer:

c. Hebrews 11 speaks of Old Testament saints who persevered in faith until they saw the will of God done on earth. What does that chapter tell you about assurance?
Answer:

d. A believer should not depend on the phrase, "once saved; always saved" for assurance of salvation. Why not according to this study?
Answer:

e. The author gives three reasons for a faith that pleases God; these three reasons generate assurance. Briefly, what are the three reasons?
Answer:

f. According to Hebrews 11, what is the assurance of things hoped for?
Answer:

g. The Old Testament saints listed in this chapter believed what two fundament truths?
Answers:
1.
2.

h. In what way does the Holy Spirit help us with the assurance of our salvation?
    Answers:

i. When prayers are answered, one's relationship with God is validated, as is one's assurance of salvation. However, to have prayers answered, one must possess a particular character trait as was found in Mary (the mother of Jesus), Zachariah and Elizabeth (parents of John the Baptist), and other Old Testament heroes of the faith. What is that character trait?
    Answer:

j. Write out Romans 8:28 (be sure to memorize it!)
    Answer:

Summary:

What stands out for you in Chapter 12? What will help you in your walk with the Lord? Write your thoughts below.

ABOUT THE AUTHOR

J im Riccitelli earned a diploma in theology from Nyack College, Nyack, NY, a diploma from the Alliance Française (Paris, France) for studies in the French language, and bachelor's and master's degrees in Sociology from the University of Toledo. His thesis (1978) addressed the social and cultural setting of rock and roll. His interest was its effect on church music.

He was ordained by The Christian and Missionary Alliance in 1950, and enjoyed pastoral experience prior to serving as an international worker. He served in ministry 45 years after retiring from service abroad. He has had extensive experience in counseling and his book, You May Now Kiss the Bride—Biblical principles for Lifelong Marital Happiness[1], presents practical application of those principles. He is committed to Biblical solutions to social—especially, relational—problems

As international workers, Jim and his wife, Ruth, served in Burkina Faso, West Africa (1950-1967), where he reduced the Red Bobo language (now called Bwamu) to writing and prepared a first draft of most of the New Testament and the book of Jonah. Additionally, they prepared literacy materials and a hymnal that required tune-tone correspondence. The Bible Societies published his article on "Tone Analysis of the Bwamu Language" in their quarterly journal. [2]

When they returned to the United States, Jim served three years as minister of music at First Alliance in Toledo, Ohio. Following that he served four years as interim pastor at the First United Presbyterian Church (Toledo, Ohio), twenty-eight years as founding pastor of The Berean Fellowship of the Church at Toledo (Toledo, Ohio), and six years as interim pastor, assistant

---

[1] WestBow Press, 1997
[2] The Bible Translator, Vol. 16, No.2, April 1965, pages 54-73

pastor, and then elder emeritus of Bethany Community Fellowship, Sylvania, Ohio.

He served as an adjunct professor at the University of Toledo, Adrian College (Adrian, Michigan), Detroit Bible College: Toledo Extension (later called Toledo's Center for Biblical Studies), and Detroit Bible College that eventually became William Tyndale College (Farmington Hills, Michigan).

He and his wife Ruth have been married sixty-nine years. They have five children, eighteen grandchildren and six great-grandchildren.

email contact: bethanyjmr@aol.com
website: www.bathostheos.com

Printed in the United States
By Bookmasters